SUMMER

An Eclectic Anthology of

Poetry & Prose

SUMMER

An Eclectic Anthology of Poetry & Prose

EDITED BY
MELANIE VILLINES

CONTRIBUTING EDITORS
JOAN JOBE SMITH
EDDIE WOODS

SILVER BIRCH PRESS
LOS ANGELES, CALIFORNIA

ISBN-13: 9780615784397

ISBN-10: 0615784399

FIRST EDITION, JUNE 2013

Email: silver@silverbirchpress.com

Web: silverbirchpress.com

Blog: silverbirchpress.wordpress.com

Book Design: Silver Birch Press

Cover and Interior Art: Odilon Redon, French Symbolist artist (1840-1916)

Mailing Address:
Silver Birch Press
P.O. Box 29458
Los Angeles, CA 90029

The Silver Birch Press
SUMMER ANTHOLOGY
is dedicated to
F. Scott Fitzgerald

INTRODUCTION

MELANIE VILLINES

As children or teens, many of us avoided the annual summer reading list—books our teachers said we should read during our vacation. We told ourselves we'd attempt these literary masterworks later—much later. Certainly not when we got out of school in June. By July we were making excuses—holidays, birthday parties, trips to the pool—and by August we'd put off any pretense of checking off even one book from the list. As adults, though, many of us spend a good part of each day reading and writing, and we've become our own advisors, making summer reading lists for ourselves—to attempt an always-meant-to-read classic (or two or three), gobble up a couple of bestsellers and not feel guilty about it, or reread some of our all-time favorites.

To me, *The Great Gatsby* by F. Scott Fitzgerald is the quintessential summer book—it takes place from June through September 1922, is easy to read, and offers that aching romantic nostalgia that is at the heart of summer. And, for this reason, we dedicate the Silver Birch Press *Summer Anthology* to F. Scott Fitzgerald. To quote my favorite passage, the opening of chapter three: "There was music from my neighbor's house through the summer nights. In his blue gardens men and girls came and went like moths among the whisperings and the champagne and the stars." Summer writing—or any writing—doesn't get any better than that.

The *Summer Anthology* is the third installment in the Silver Birch Press anthology series—after the *Silver Anthology* (November 2012) and the *Green Anthology* (March 2013). In this edition, we explore all things summer—a season that holds most of our memories, our hopes, our dreams, and a time when we reveled in fun and freedom. In the *Summer Anthology,* we revisit summers past, childhood, loves won and lost, the great outdoors, travel, magical evenings, hopeful mornings, and most of all we remember the heat—in all of its many forms. (Thanks to contributing editor Eddie Woods for suggesting "Light & Dark" as a section title.)

In the *Summer Anthology,* you'll find poetry, prose poems, short stories, novel excerpts, memoirs, and essays from over seventy writers around the world—authors I invited to participate or writers invited by contributing editors Joan Jobe Smith and Eddie Woods or a fellow contributor. Also included in the collection are a number of classic authors: William Blake, Anton Chekhov, Paul Laurence Dunbar, Edna St. Vincent Millay, Carl Sandburg, William Shakespeare, Robert Louis Stevenson, and Edith Wharton.

The *Summer Anthology* differs in several ways from our previous anthologies—including a larger format (7x10) and changes in typography. We hope these revisions will give us more breathing room and make the collection more reader friendly. In selecting artwork, we tried many different approaches, but decided to feature paintings by Odilon Redon because the style of this French Surrealist painter seemed magical, dreamy, light, airy, and, well…summery.

Thank you for taking this summer journey with us. Happy reading!

"And so with the sunshine and the great bursts of leaves growing on the trees, just as things grow in fast movies, I had that familiar conviction that life was beginning over again with the summer."

F. SCOTT FITZGERALD, *The Great Gatsby*

CONTENTS

SILVER BIRCH PRESS
SUMMER ANTHOLOGY

PART I
SEASON

TAMARA MADISON

Summer

June is Friday: weary of winter
exhausted by spring, brightened
by hope of rest and warmth
and green things stretching
toward the dear sun of summer.

July, then, is Saturday:
brown-limbed, easy, moving slow
through the long hours
of sand, of fish lifted
by clear waves with the light
shining through, of warm
nights with Mars glowing
gold near the rocking moon.

August, alas, must be Sunday:
there's still time, the days
still balmy and long
the sun still hot, Mars still
bright in the warm night sky,
the sea still glittering
with the coins of the sun.
But the shadow at the end
looms longer every day.

And then it's September:
a cheap and painful parody
of summer: hotter than August
but the days grow shorter
and we are stuck wherever
we have to be as wild fires
devour the hills of spring
leaving us pining for July

when time stretched out
on a blanket before us,
naked and smiling.

CHRIS FORHAN

Oh Blessed Season

Summer strode slowly in clownish festoonery, forgiving everything.

Blessed was the fruit of its womb: slumbering bees, blossoms' furious purple effusions,
clouds scattered like napkins late of lips moist with cream and champagne.

Chiffon was a word heard often then.

Oh, to live like that again, operatically bored with the reckless long business of becoming.

To loll on a ridge above the jostling gondolas,
to sprawl in a field amid the ruins of lunch, the crumbs and rinds,
to be slaked by a final swallow of wine and feel safely ravaged and awry,

to joy in the horses' forelocks, beribboned with blooms of sweet everlasting—
a distraction from the black, inapt cast of their eyes,

that sequestered look, as of something they've seen and not forgotten yet.

Originally published in *Slate*.

CHRIS FORHAN

Hopeful Green Stuff

We'd been issued our folk guitars and fake books, striped pants and puka shell bracelets.

Summer's vast expanse unfurling, bare feet stained green by the fresh-cut grass, fingers contorting toward the major chords.

Wasps thronged the melon balls, brambles strangled the garden. We turned golden.

O lush boredom, blue extravagant sky, transistor insisting *Someday we'll walk in the rays of a beautiful sun...*

Moms were there, pouring chilled milk. When dark descended, dads raised flames in the pit.

We circled it, we sang along, there was nothing we were learning. We were earning our ribbons for participation.

Originally published in *Black Leapt In* (Barrow Street, 2009)

CHRIS FORHAN

The Church of the Backyard

Delores wears her celery-colored
swimming suit, the one embellished
with tiny slices of watermelon,
a bite out of each of them.

Assuredly seven, she's eighteen months
and one day older than Ronald, who trips
and sprawls again in the gravel. Last Tuesday
that trick earned a popsicle.

Our newly teenaged sister Vicki
suns herself and paints her toenails green
to match her plastic sandals. Starting today,
she proclaims, we are to call her Victoria.

Mother wears her summer hat: the wide
fried egg that shades her paperback
and wobbles around her ears whenever
she laughs or lifts her head to speak

to father: first one in the pool,
first time out of a business suit
all season, splayed on his inner tube,
circling the deep end, orchid-white.

I've got my Batman outfit on
and, stern-jawed, saunter across the lawn
wearing the others' admiration
lightly. Who would say

through all the little deaths, the separations,
all the long untidy years to come,
each unholy ruckus (the wine glass
smashed against the wall in anger, fists

that pound the steering wheel, bodies
sitting bolt upright in bed with night sweats),
who would say, through all of this,
we're not redeemed by our essential silliness?

From *Forgive Us Our Happiness* (University Press of New England, 1999)

KIRSTEN DIERKING

The Ordinary

It's summer, so
 the pink gingham shorts,
the red mower, the neat rows
of clean smelling grass
unspooling behind
the sweeping blades.

A dragonfly, black body
big as a finger, will not leave
the mower alone,
loving the sparkle
of scarlet metal,
seeing in even a rusting paint
the shade of a flower.

But I wave him off,
conscious he is
wasting his time,
conscious I am
filling my time
with such small details,
distracting colors,

Like pink checks,
like this, then that,
Like a dragonfly wing
in the sun reflecting
the color of opals,
like all the hours
we leave behind,
so ordinary,
but not unloved.

From *Northern Oracle*. © Spout Press, 2007. Reprinted with permission.

A Rhyme for Summertime

I'm looking for a rhyme for summertime
That would convey how summer play
Is special fun with warmth and sun
A sweet respite from winter's night.

Since early maturation summer signifies vacation,
Your feet hit the ground, desk and couch unbound,
Hat nor coat, unfettered; summer reading not lettered,
Making plans into the night, inspired by the light,
Smiles, less despair, with flowers everywhere
Till with no regret for mosquitoes or for sweat
You look backward on it all and forward to the fall.

THOMAS R. THOMAS

barefoot days—building
up my feet to take the black
asphalt-shards of glass

embedded in my sole—cool
drink sip, lazy in the sun

VIRGINIE COLLINE

Summer Haiku

Spanish summertime
a living frieze of seagulls
against the blue sky

the rocks in the waves
a pod of petrified whales
awaiting the sun

seashell lullaby
dark blue memories of you
whisper in my ear

the sky above us
skin languorously sun-kissed
a murmur of silk

starry canopy
the moon is sitting pretty
on the summer's throne

LORI McGINN

When Summer Arrives Dressed in Red

i will stuff her in my backpack
hike to the other side of the moon
kick her rebel mouth to the dust

when i was a teen i would get high
let the sun have its way with me
it would scorch my sleepy cells

i am a crisp crumbling dreamer
tree shadow arms lull me into their web

now there are marshmallow fields
a sticky white world of marshmallows
this is how my world is now

i dream of roses
i am baked
i eat clouds

DIANE WAKOSKI

Summer

she slid out of the skin, leaving it
like a dried lima bean hull,
white and papery on the road.
her body inched along
the highway,
rippling its new red colors
bits of brown
like stones
seemed strewn along each arm and thigh.
it was a strange transformation
which had been coming.
the moon had warned her flipping like a fish in the sky,
a bowl of sweet cream left overnight emptied itself to the snake
living under the hearth.
when the time had come the old skin had shucked off
crackling, no pain
no pulling. she slid her wet body into the sun.
she was dry now
and brown.
the ocean rushed through her head; she heard crabs
moving sideways on the bottom
and the fish
shouting
with their fins.

First published in *The New Yorker* and reprinted in *Inside the Blood Factory* (Doubleday, 1968)

PAUL LAURENCE DUNBAR

In Summer

Oh, summer has clothed the earth
In a cloak from the loom of the sun!
And a mantle, too, of the skies' soft blue,
And a belt where the rivers run.
And now for the kiss of the wind,
And the touch of the air's soft hands,
With the rest from strife and the heat of life,
With the freedom of lakes and lands.
I envy the farmer's boy
Who sings as he follows the plow;
While the shining green of the young blades lean
To the breezes that cool his brow.
He sings to the dewy morn,
No thought of another's ear;
But the song he sings is a chant for kings
And the whole wide world to hear.
He sings of the joys of life,
Of the pleasures of work and rest,
From an o'erfull heart, without aim or art;
'Tis a song of the merriest.
O ye who toil in the town,
And ye who moil in the mart,
Hear the artless song, and your faith made strong
Shall renew your joy of heart.
Oh, poor were the worth of the world
If never a song were heard—
If the sting of grief had no relief,
And never a heart were stirred.
So, long as the streams run down,
And as long as the robins trill,
Let us taunt old Care with a merry air,
And sing in the face of ill.

WILLIAM BLAKE

To Summer

O thou who passest thro' our valleys in
Thy strength, curb thy fierce steeds, allay the heat
That flames from their large nostrils! thou, O Summer,
Oft pitched'st here thy golden tent, and oft
Beneath our oaks hast slept, while we beheld
With joy thy ruddy limbs and flourishing hair.

Beneath our thickest shades we oft have heard
Thy voice, when noon upon his fervid car
Rode o'er the deep of heaven; beside our springs
Sit down, and in our mossy valleys, on

Some bank beside a river clear, throw thy
Silk draperies off, and rush into the stream:
Our valleys love the Summer in his pride.

Our bards are fam'd who strike the silver wire:
Our youth are bolder than the southern swains:
Our maidens fairer in the sprightly dance:
We lack not songs, nor instruments of joy,
Nor echoes sweet, nor waters clear as heaven,
Nor laurel wreaths against the sultry heat

PART II
DAYS & NIGHTS

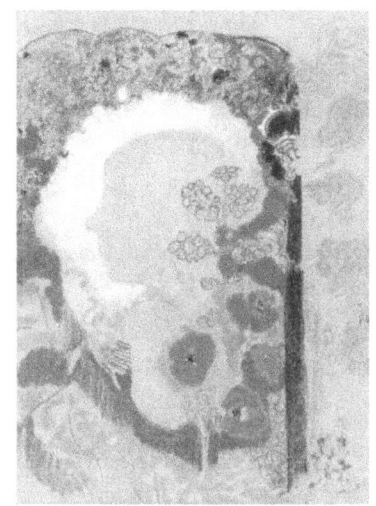

WILLIAM SHAKESPEARE

Sonnet 18

Shall I compare thee to a summer's day?
Thou art more lovely and more temperate:
Rough winds do shake the darling buds of May,
And summer's lease hath all too short a date:
Sometime too hot the eye of heaven shines,
And often is his gold complexion dimm'd;
And every fair from fair sometime declines,
By chance or nature's changing course untrimm'd;
But thy eternal summer shall not fade
Nor lose possession of that fair thou owest;
Nor shall Death brag thou wander'st in his shade,
When in eternal lines to time thou growest:
So long as men can breathe or eyes can see,
So long lives this and this gives life to thee.

Thomas R. Thomas

AM Radio

Those were the days when
I would lay in bed and
listen as the AM clock radio
would play "Light My Fire,"
and "Everybody's Talkin,"
and "(Sittin' On) The Dock of the Bay,"
happy that I could stay
in bed all morning smoking
my cigarettes in bed.

Then I would waste the rest
of the day listening to
my albums on the living
room stereo, The Rolling Stones,
Pink Floyd, and Neil Young,

until evening when we would
all meet at the corner of
the cemetery smoking cigarettes
and joints, and playing
hide and seek behind the
headstones,

hoping I can find out
if my pretty neighbor's
cousin really stuffed
Kleenex in her bra,

then at midnight lay in
bed waiting for two
hours daydreaming of
cigarettes, and joints,
and girls—listening
as the AM radio plays
all night in my ear.

DANIEL ROMO

Last Summer

We ran Ibex Avenue—
courting the dusk and
counting crickets,
before our mothers called us inside
in three different languages
for a late dinner.

Paul called everyone *dickhead* that year.
And Tony kissed all three of the Hernandez girls,
even Eva with the mole on her neck
shaped like a churro.

On Saturdays we bounced
a lopsided rubber basketball
in my fissured driveway,
trampling my senile neighbor's begonias,
then drank from her tired hose
letting the water dribble down our scrawny chests
before tossing it aside,
proudly looking up to the neon August sky
palms outstretched as if
we were gods.

When seduced by the incantations
of the Indian ice cream man,
we ran inside our homes, gathering change
to buy Mexican candies
made with trace amounts of lead,
and sweet cigarettes
with powdered sugar tips.

We didn't call each other *fags*
for enticing the ladybugs to crawl up our fingertips.
We saved bravado for our dads,
who cursed the TV when the Dodgers lost.

We even cried when I moved away.
I hear Paul has testicular cancer now.
Tony is paying alimony to four exes.
But we were bad asses then—

lying on rooftops,
humming the song of the ice cream man,
puffing away
on candy cigs.

Originally published in *Camroc Press Review*

—

DANIEL ROMO

Stickball
> *For Jerry*

Summers were a never-ending 7th inning,
and games stretched into the next day
when the sun no longer lit the cul-de-sac.

My brother's knuckleball was an
experiment in flight pattern,
a taunting array of speculation:

       juking and jutting,
  a hovering slow-dance
               inventing new steps
the batter could never learn.

My fastball was a humming blur of rocket science.

And whoever made contact deserved to
commandeer the moon.

The neighborhood kids were filler.

Portuguese soccer-playing
perpetual strikeout victims
always stuck out in right field,
because they were more skilled with their feet
than with their hands.

Today it's the bottom of the 9th inning.
Two outs.

And we are dreamers posing as fathers
reminding our own children,
"Point your toe to the target.
Keep your elbow up.
And follow through on the pitch."

Today I remember belting an old tennis ball
over the neighbor's roof
into his backyard,
gliding around makeshift bases
with glorious fists raised
as if God was pulling our hands.

      Originally published in *decomP*.

WILLIAM BLAKE

The Schoolboy

I love to rise in a summer morn,
When the birds sing on every tree;
The distant huntsman winds his horn,
And the skylark sings with me.
O! what sweet company.

But to go to school in a summer morn,
O! it drives all joy away;
Under a cruel eye outworn.
The little ones spend the day,
In sighing and dismay.

Ah! then at times I drooping sit,
And spend many an anxious hour,
Nor in my book can I take delight,
Nor sit in learnings bower,
Worn thro' with the dreary shower.

How can the bird that is born for joy,
Sit in a cage and sing.
How can a child when fears annoy.
But droop his tender wing.
And forget his youthful spring.

O! father & mother. if buds are nip'd,
And blossoms blown away,
And if the tender plants are strip'd
Of their joy in the springing day,
By sorrow and care's dismay.

How shall the summer arise in joy.
Or the summer fruits appear.
Or how shall we gather what griefs destroy
Or bless the mellowing year.
When the blasts of winter appear.

PAUL LAURENCE DUNBAR

A Boy's Summer Song

'Tis fine to play
In the fragrant hay,
And romp on the golden load;
To ride old Jack
To the barn and back,
Or tramp by a shady road.
To pause and drink,
At a mossy brink;
Ah, that is the best of joy,
And so I say
On a summer's day,
What's so fine as being a boy?
Ha, Ha!
With line and hook
By a babbling brook,
The fisherman's sport we ply;
And list the song
Of the feathered throng
That flit in the branches nigh.
At last we strip
For a quiet dip;
Ah, that is the best of joy.
For this I say
On a summer's day,
What's so fine as being a boy?
Ha, Ha

BRUCE WEIGL

Pastoral as Complaint

The robin is so quarrelsome. He barks to no one in the trees;
he fluffs his body twice its size and rattles in the leaves.
　He doesn't know or won't accept the nest is empty now,
the eggs a tatter on the ground. The storm was quick,
　we didn't see it come; no sound above the hum

a summer morning makes when god is in his place
　and we are free of tragedies that pile up along the way.
The robin is so quarrelsome;
　he thinks his life is gone just like the nest,
but he's like the rest of us, it's only just begun.

Previously published in *The Abundance of Nothing* (*Triquarterly*, 2012)

BRUCE WEIGL

Apparition of the Exile

There was another life of cool summer mornings, the dogwood air and the slag stink so gray like our monsoon which we loved for the rain and cool wind until the rot came into us. And I remember the boys we were the evening of our departure, our mothers waving through the train's black pluming exhaust; they were not proud in their tears of our leaving, so don't tell me to shut up about the war or I might pull something from my head, from my head, from my head that you wouldn't want to see and whoever the people are might be offended.

From the green country you reconstruct in your brain, from the rubble and stink of your occupation, there is no moving out. A sweet boy who got drunk and brave on our long ride into the State draws a maze every day on white paper, precisely in his room of years as if you could walk into it. All day he draws and imagines his platoon will return from the burning river where he sent them sixteen years ago into fire. He can't stop seeing the line of trees explode in white phosphorous blossoms and the liftship sent for them spinning uncontrollably beyond hope into the Citadel wall. Only his mother comes these days, drying the fruit in her apron or singing the cup of hot tea into his fingers which, like barbed wire, web the air.

Previously published in *Archaeology of the Circle: New and Selected Poems* (Grove/Atlantic, 1999)

CATFISH MCDARIS

All I Know Is I Love You

In the shadow
ochre pewter dawn

Arms legs lips
smiles hair hips
tangled sheets

I don't want
to shut my eyes
without you

Or ever open them
again unless I know
you'll be there

Where ever you are
I wish to be there
never alone again.

CONRAD ROMO

Cement God

We're in the middle of a heat wave. Every window in our house is wide open to coax any kinda merciful breeze that might happen to crawl by. As soon as I open my eyes I brace myself, remembering yesterday's scorcher and the day before that and the day before that. The temperature has been getting over a hundred and you just know it's gonna be another hot one.

But this early morning, it's almost cool and amazingly quiet. No sounds of snorin', no sounds from the radio or TV, no horns honkin' or tires screechin' or people yellin', no birds squawkin' or dogs barkin' or cats fightin' or babies cryin' or noise from the train yards or factories at the end of the street. Nothing except for the hum of the refrigerator.

I know it won't last, though, this quiet and the slight cool air of the morning, but I just want to hold onto it and make it stretch. It's like some kind of a truce, some sort of settlement has been reached in our house and on our block and in our neighborhood. But I know it can't last.

Maybe someone else, one of my brothers or sisters or my mom or dad, is awake too, like me, just lying still in their beds. They might even be pretending to sleep. We do a lot of pretending, my family does. We pretend to know things we don't and to not know things we do. We pretend what matters, doesn't, and that we don't care about the things we honestly do. We pretend things that aren't funny are and that we get the joke when we don't. And we pretend to have a plan and that we know our lines.

So who knows if it's real or pretend sleep that has them all still and quiet but I seize this moment to dress in a hurry and sneak outside. I stand barefoot and stretch at the bottom of our back porch stairs by the banana tree that shades the imprints of feet in the cement. I put a foot in the impression of my big cousin Juno, trying to imagine him when he was my age and our feet were the same size. Alongside his footprints are those of his sister Rachel and the hand and footprints of my older sister Letty and cousins Linda and Dickie and a date scratched in the cement from a time before I was born.

I stretch and look at the cloudless sky and walk down the driveway toward my grandparents' house. The cement is still cool, but in a few hours I'll need chanclas or something to keep my feet from frying.

My granddad owns this property. The front and the back houses plus another down the street where my uncle Pete and his family live. My granddad built the *back* house where I live. Friends and family helped with the carpentry, plumbing, and electrical, but the cement work, that was all his. The foundation, the porches and stairs, the long driveway and the wide yard between the houses were all done by his hand. In fact he did most of the cement work that could be done on our block. He was best as a finisher, the guy responsible for smoothing and leveling the pour. When he was done, there'd be just enough of a grade that water wouldn't ever pool. He was never without work, not even during the depression in the thirties.

But I didn't know any of that then as I walked from the back to the front house. It was long before I was alive, so how could I have known? I didn't know then how he came to have a limp and needed a cane to walk. Years later I learned that he was cleaning the walls and blades inside a big commercial cement mixer when someone accidentally hit a switch, starting the blades spinning in opposite directions. He was cut badly before his cries were heard and the machine shut down.

I didn't know any of this then as I worked my way to the front house, having nothing particular in mind. I didn't know much of anything then and wondered years later if anyone would remember seeing a boy walking with an old man in his piss-stained pants and beat-up hat, one hand on the boy's shoulder and the other on a cane moving slowly, inch by inch along the sidewalk he had poured and made smooth. Would anyone remember them walking to Pierre's Liquor Store to get the old man a couple bottles of muscatel past the walls made of river rock and across Cypress Avenue where people in their cars honked impatiently as the two slowly crossed?

The boy glared back at them—a dare to keep on honking. In years to come, they'd never remember the kid and the old borracho, the old drunk. Why give them a second thought?

That summer, though, that summer morning I found Granddad sitting on a rocker smoking a freshly rolled cigarette from his can of Prince Albert tobacco.

"Hola PANZÓN," he said. His nickname for me cause I'm kinda fat.

"Hola Abuelo," I said and sat with my back to him on the green painted cement steps of his front porch and pointed my face toward the sun, looking at the veins through my closed eyelids at a blood-red world as the rays caressed my face. There are some things you are just not supposed to look at directly.

Then again, you just can't rely on your eyes to tell you everything. That morning in the company of my granddad and in no rush to see the summer unfold, there was a contained richness. There was only the up and down of the heavens and the earth. Or in this case, the holy cement beneath my feet.

Some kids may have asked the basic questions of their grandfathers. "Granddad, why's the sky blue and the sun yellow or where do clouds and babies come from and what was I before I was born?" But not me. Not when the mystery was right there beneath my feet.

And so I asked, "Granddad, who made the sidewalks?"

And he answered right back at me without pause, "I did."

And I didn't breathe for a few seconds or it could have been minutes. That's when I knew my granddad was God. I don't remember either one of us saying anything after that. Really, what was there to say? I mean just a moment before he was only my granddad, a mere mortal, an old piss-pants boracho and now I'm different and he is so much more.

IVON PREFONTAINE

Poetry Written

Sit quietly,
5:30
AM.
Can't sleep
wait
listen
pay attention
be patient
meditate
contemplate
focus on breath.
Gently return
to a quiet space
solitude
like a river
single words
phrases form
metaphors arise
images appear
in the current.
Discover a gentle smile
on the corners of lips
face softens.
Fresh day
creates space
for voice
words observed
soul speaks
a summer breeze refreshes
asks to be heard.
Tranquil,
bump into creative moment.

Summer Magic

Crawling quietly from his tent,
His dad still lost in slumber within,
He sits down alone on the granite slab,
Coltish legs drawn up to his chin,
And arms wrapped around skinny knees.
He gazes toward the pale horizon,
Watching the sleeping valley below.
With breath held in anticipation,
He waits for the magic
He knows will come.

There! A thin curve of molten red!
A far away sliver of fiery light
Breaks the horizon.
Rising slowly,
It bathes the tops of the rolling hills
In a brilliant spill of gold.
Mother-of-pearl dawn
Gives way to butter yellow
Morning light.

In front of his wide, blue eyes,
The world awakens.
Magic arrives and
Day is born,
Again.
He smiles to himself and wraps
His arms more tightly
Around his knees,
Shivering in private delight, and
Holding the beauty
Close within,
Having already learned
Some magic is
Secret.

CAITLIN STERN

Word Vacation

Lazy sun-drenched afternoon
scramble up a tree
the trunk a ship's mast
book clenched between teeth
a pirate's sword
In that lofty
leafy perch
shaded by spreading branches
sail on the page-waves
to exotic climes
windswept white sand beaches
fire-lit den in a ivy-clad manor home
gleaming spaceship corridors
far from the scorching heat
for an hour or two

Julie Cadwallader-Staub

Reverence

The air vibrated
with the sound of cicadas
on those hot Missouri nights after sundown
when the grown-ups gathered on the wide back lawn,
sank into their slung-back canvas chairs
tall glasses of iced tea beading in the heat

and we sisters chased fireflies
reaching for them in the dark
admiring their compact black bodies
their orange stripes and seeking antennas
as they crawled to our fingertips
and clicked open into the night air.

In all the days and years that have followed,
I don't know that I've ever experienced
that same utter certainty of the goodness of life
that was as palpable
as the sound of the cicadas on those nights:

my sisters running around with me in the dark,
the murmur of the grown-ups' voices,
the way reverence mixes with amazement
to see such a small body
emit so much light.

From *Friends Journal*. ©Religious Society of Friends. Reprinted with permission.

TED KOOSER

A Summer Night

At the end of the street
a porch light is burning,
showing the way. How simple,
how perfect it seems: the darkness,
the white house like a passage
through summer and into
a snowfield. Night after night,
the lamp comes on at dusk,
the end of the street
stands open and white,
and an old woman sits there tending the lonely gate.

From *Flying at Night: Poems 1965-1985* (University of Pittsburgh Press, 2005)

IVON PREFONTAINE

Summer Ends

He lit down oh so gently
He posed oh so perfectly.
I had him say;
I really did!
"Take my picture please
My time almost done
This serves as a final memorial."
I took his picture
He stood oh so still
Posed oh so gratefully
Once done, he took his leave, gracefully
Both our jobs nearly done.

DANIEL PATRICK DELANEY

Summer Nights and the Short Wave Radio

I stop and listen for anyone coming, before stepping over the *Playboy* magazines scattered across the floor that I look at during the day near the side of my cousin John's bed. I take a cigarette butt out of the full ashtray on the cluttered bureau and straighten it out, before lighting it. My face glows in the mirror then fades with the match and in that second I see myself as a man. I take one long drag and then put it out, just to get the taste in my mouth, before pulling a single cigarette from a crumpled pack next to the ashtray.

I had my first smoke when I'm six years old, but now I'm eight and think about having one all day long at school. Now that it's Summer I like to keep an open pack in my pocket, just three or four cigarettes with a pack of matches. I know if Aunt Kate catches me she'll beat me bad. I have that thought in the pit of my stomach each time I light one, but I don't want to stop. None of my friends smoke, I do it alone and don't tell anyone. Squeezing through the propped-up door, I stand still at the top of the third-floor steps to wait for a sound, any sound to tell me if I'm caught.

The big wind-up clock on the Florida orange crate next to my bed ticks away with the slight sound of the alarm bells jingling, just waiting to go off. I slip the soft white cigarette under the pillow and then wind the metal clock. Aunt Kate doesn't wake me up in the morning, not even for school, so I have to use the clock. It makes me feel like I don't need her for anything. John shows me how to make my bed like he did in the Marines—it's flat and smooth and I can bounce a quarter off of it. With my white boxers on and my buzzed head, I feel like I'm in the Marines.

In the smoldering hot kitchen in the middle of the day, Aunt Kate digs the electric buzzer into my head and tells me, "We don't need any towheads around here. Your blonde hair reminds me of your goddamn father." I watch the yellow-white hair fall to the floor against the black and white checkered tiles, and I'm glad I remind her of my dad, who I don't even know. With little pieces of hair stuck all over my clammy body, I stare back at Aunt Kate when she's done and pretend I'm my father looking at her. It makes me feel like I have the power of a grown man over her.

I ease open the top drawer of the old, heavy bureau and pull out a can of lemon furniture polish that I take from the kitchen. Shaking the can, I feel just enough to polish my short wave radio that sits on top of the bureau. In the dark, I rub the polish into the hard wood. I go over the entire radio, covering every inch without looking away. The scent of the lemon mixes with the sweet smell of the wood and leaves the taste of an orange peel on my tongue. I wrap the near empty can with the old cloth that is stained and worn from polish and wood, then place it back into the drawer. It gives me the quiet feeling of cleaning the challis like Father Duffy, after communion. Father Duffy isn't like the other priests, being a fullback at Notre Dame and all. He even smokes and curses like a real man. I'd like to be like him someday, even if it means being a priest.

—

In the darkened room with just the radio on, I place both hands on the top of the wooden box and wait for it to come to life. The tubes in the radio start to heat up and smell like the old black iron that I use every morning to iron my clothes before school. The sound of the neighbors' air conditioners hum next door, as the broken box fan rattles away in John's window, even though he's not home. He's at the Velvet Lounge.

After supper, I'm shinning his shoes and he gives me five dollars and a pack of matches that is covered in red velvet. It has a phone number on it and a lady with long black gloves on the inside cover. "This is where I'll be if you need me," he says with a grin on his face. He's dressed in a black suit with a white tie and looks like James Bond. The smell of his cologne is on the match pack and I wish I was old enough to go with him. I don't even wait for Aunt Kate to ask for the money John gives me for shinning his shoes anymore, I just hand it over, but I keep the matches. She'll stick her hands right in my pockets, so I put the match pack in the elastic of my underwear like a POW. I think of myself like that, like the POWs I see on TV in Vietnam. At night in the summer, the heat of the third floor is like an oven. I'm moving the dial of the short wave radio with the dog tags that John gives me hanging from my neck, pretending to be listening for news of the outside world. I listen to the sound of what I think are Chinese voices and tell myself they're up to no good. The sweat starts to roll down the beaded links of the chain that hold the dog tags around my neck, so I take it off and lower them into a sock in the top drawer, before changing the band on the radio back to A.M.

Through the whistling and static, the chatter of Connie Mack Stadium begins to fill the room—and I realize it's after eight and the Phillies are on.

I climb onto the coolness of the flat sheets and lay my head back. As it sinks into the feather pillow, I start to think about walking out of the house and going down to the game all by myself. I've been there twice with John and I know I can do it. I picture myself taking the bus to the trolley stop and then the trolley to the subway, all the way to the stadium. I'll sit right behind home plate, that's were Uncle Lenny says the rich people sit. I remember me and John getting up out of our seats on the subway to let two black ladies sit down and how they smile at me and I smile back the whole way, as we hold on to the pole, rocking back and forth. When they call us real gentlemen I stand up straight like John, as the lights flicker on and off. It's already the top of the third and I know it will have to wait, just for tonight.

In a flash, my mind switches to playing shortstop and pitching for Little League. I'm Bobby Wine or Chris Short on the Phillies. I field and bat like Bobby Wine. When I'm on the mound, I pitch like Chris Short. Most of the other kids are fumbling around out there, but not me—I do what they do and it works. I play like a man, and they're just little boys. I just tell one kid about it, Tommy Braun, our catcher, but he thinks he's Johnny Bench, that's how good he is. Tommy says he wishes I was Tom Seaver instead of Chris Short.

Tommy's mom and dad are nice, nicer than Tommy, and they give me a ride to all of our baseball practices and games and I even eat dinner at their house, but I don't tell Aunt Kate. It's not his real dad, but he's the best I ever saw. Uncle Lenny doesn't give me a ride to anything, no one is even allowed in the house. Tommy's dad coaches baseball and takes us to get ice cream after every game, win or lose. Their house is so big and clean and he has everything, even a TV in his own room. I'd still rather have the short wave radio, but he doesn't understand that and he won't ever see it, cause he can't come in the house. I tell him about my real dad and how he's gonna come to our next game. I still look for him during every game, but by now we both know he's not coming. I know it's a lie, but I have to say it. Tommy never mentions it… Sometimes I pretend my dad is at the game and I try to be perfect. I'll be there like all of the other dads for real when my son is playing baseball. I promise my son that and he's not even born yet, but I tell him just the same.

I start to imagine myself playing for the Phillies and By Saum saying, with his deep voice, "And now batting for the Phillies, number seven, shortstop, Danny Delaney." And getting a standing ovation every time. Even Aunt Kate will have to watch on the big TV when I'm playing for the Phillies. She wants me to call her mom, but I don't call her anything. She asks me "What's your name?" and I say "Danny Delaney" every time, then she smacks me in the head with her rings turned around until I say "Danny Conway." In ten more years I'll be eighteen and change my name back to Delaney, and that'll make her sick for sure. She will have to hear my name over and over again and each time it will be like a whip on her back. The thought of it tickles my stomach.

Uncle Lenny's voice is getting closer, he's saying good night and coming up the steps laughing to himself. The same laugh that turns to a cold dead stare in an instant. I slide off the bed as fast as I can and turn off the radio. He's stopped at the hallway that leads to the third floor. I can hear his bodyweight shifting back and forth on the loose floorboards and him breathing. I stand frozen in front of the radio. He starts, then stops, before heading for the bathroom. I think he's weak because he hesitates. Aunt Kate never hesitates. I like to think of them as two little kids living in my house, so I can beat them, but the man I see myself as, with the reddish blonde beard and blue eyes, can't do it, not even to those two.

A long deep breath shutters through me and then my hand is on the black knob. The sound of a click cuts me in half, as I climb back on to the bed and reach for the cigarette under my pillow. My fingertips brush the smooth velvet pack of matches along with the loose cigarette. I lie back, my leg crossed above my knee smoking an unlit cigarette, with the radio down low. While blowing imaginary smoke rings into the muggy night, I rub the velvet match pack and picture myself sitting right next to John in the Velvet Lounge…

STANLEY PLUMLY

Sitting Alone in the Middle of the Night

Maybe it was summer and I was back home for a while
working to pay off debts from school, painting white
barns and long field fences and on off-days baling hay.
It was hot then in Ohio and sometimes so dry the corn
or the soybeans would fail. I'd get up at two or three
 in the morning to find my way to the kitchen for water
and he'd be sitting there in a kind of outline,
smoking and staring at something far, his eyes by now
long adjusted to the dark. Mine were just now opening.
Nothing would be said, since there was nothing to say.
He was dying, he was turning into stone. The little
I could see I could see already how much heavier
he made the air, heavy enough over the days that
          summer
you could feel in the house the pull of the earth.

From *Orphan Hours*. © W.W. Norton & Company, 2012.

ROBERT LOUIS STEVENSON

Bed in Summer

In winter I get up at night
And dress by yellow candlelight.
In summer, quite the other way,
I have to go to bed by day.

I have to go to bed and see
The birds still hopping on the tree,
Or hear the grown-up people's feet
Still going past me in the street.

And does it not seem hard to you,
When all the sky is clear and blue,
And I should like so much to play,
To have to go to bed by day?

From *A Child's Garden of Verses,* first published in 1885

PART III
JUNE

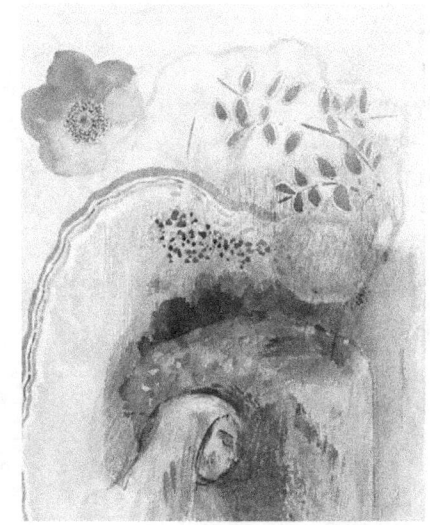

EDITH WHARTON

Summer

(*Excerpt from Chapter 1*)

A girl came out of lawyer Royall's house, at the end of the one street of North Dormer, and stood on the doorstep.

It was the beginning of a June afternoon. The springlike transparent sky shed a rain of silver sunshine on the roofs of the village, and on the pastures and larchwoods surrounding it. A little wind moved among the round white clouds on the shoulders of the hills, driving their shadows across the fields and down the grassy road that takes the name of street when it passes through North Dormer. The place lies high and in the open, and lacks the lavish shade of the more protected New England villages. The clump of weeping willows about the duck pond, and the Norway spruces in front of the Hatchard gate, cast almost the only roadside shadow between lawyer Royall's house and the point where, at the other end of the village, the road rises above the church and skirts the black hemlock wall enclosing the cemetery.

The little June wind, frisking down the street, shook the doleful fringes of the Hatchard spruces, caught the straw hat of a young man just passing under them, and spun it clean across the road into the duck-pond.

As he ran to fish it out the girl on lawyer Royall's doorstep noticed that he was a stranger, that he wore city clothes, and that he was laughing with all his teeth, as the young and careless laugh at such mishaps.

Her heart contracted a little, and the shrinking that sometimes came over her when she saw people with holiday faces made her draw back into the house and pretend to look for the key that she knew she had already put into her pocket. A narrow greenish mirror with a gilt eagle over it hung on the passage wall, and she looked critically at her reflection, wished for the thousandth time that she had blue eyes like Annabel Balch, the girl who sometimes came from Springfield to spend a week with old Miss Hatchard, straightened the sunburnt hat over her small swarthy face, and turned out again into the sunshine.

"How I hate everything!" she murmured.

The young man had passed through the Hatchard gate, and she had the street to herself. North Dormer is at all times an empty place, and at three o'clock on a June afternoon its few able-bodied men are off in the fields or woods, and the women indoors, engaged in languid household drudgery.

The girl walked along, swinging her key on a finger, and looking about her with the heightened attention produced by the presence of a stranger in a familiar place. What, she wondered, did North Dormer look like to people from other parts of the world?

DANIEL MCGINN

June Moon

Today was sheltered
in a marine layer, we waded through
a sea without shadows.

Today I made a donation
for the funeral of a friend
killed by a drunk driver.

Tonight I watched a mouse escape from my dog.
I watched pink feet and black fur blur across concrete.

Tonight I saw the moon
poke its head out from the clouds
a black mist began rising up like a cape
to cover the chin, the lips, the teeth…

Lori asked me,
Does the moon always shows us the same face
or does it sometimes show us other faces?
I don't know, I said and we marveled
at how clouds had misshapen the moon's skull.
It looked dented and pockmarked.
It looked like it had been kicked
and kicked repeatedly.

Feral kittens under my house began to yowl.
My dog ran zigzags
and barked and barked and barked.
A mouse squeezed her body into a hole in a brick wall,
a tight passage, small as a pencil spine,
then the mouse was gone.

No lights twinkled.
The moon turned dark as a dime
dropped down a slot.

CLINT MARGRAVE

Rue de Rivoli
Fête des Pères, 2008

The only time I saw my father
wear the tie I bought on this street,
was in his casket.

I had been living in Paris as a student some years ago,
and got it as a souvenir.

He never said much about it,
unwrapped the box,
held it up,
set it down on the chair next to him.

I might've felt
the same way had my son
brought me home such
a thoughtless gift from France.

At the time,
it had been the best I could afford—
and besides, what did you get a man
who didn't have any interests? I thought,
as I passed the place
where I bought it six years earlier,
when my father was alive
and there was nothing profound
about the tie or walking
the Rue de Rivoli
on Father's Day.

CAROLYN MILLER

Night of the Summer Solstice

We celebrated the solstice by a waterfall
the water overflowing like our lives rushing
and rushing past us so much water
in the narrow channel of the slanting Mousse
it fell onto the rocks and blew up in spray
and the sound of it almost drowned out our talking
as we laughed together and drank Champagne
the bubbles rising in our glasses like spray
from the rocks while everywhere leaves
were conspiring to live their lives and the stones
looked on with their histories locked inside them
and we talked on as water spilled and fell and the light
stayed on after we had left our emptied glasses
and the sound of the waterfall kept on rising
in the narrow gorge where tiny wild orchids
bloomed in the long long light and the river
begonias waited for their turn to open
in the fullness of that summer

PART IV
HEAT

Heat Wave

Sheets thrown off
sticky with sweat
I lie on the top bunk,
listen to june bugs
bounce off the screen.
My hands dance pirouettes
in the dusky light,
a charm to induce sleep.
The TV drones.
Loud voices travel.
When the front door slams
it jerks my body,
like a finger in a hot socket.

In the morning, he is gone.
She sweeps the broken glass.
I hear a crack of thunder
and the sky turns dark.
At last it rains.

MERRILL FARNSWORTH

Gabriel's Wings

Sometimes melancholy paints my mind gunmetal gray.
July's ripe mango mood kidnapped by winter.
Like Persephone I'm tangled in shadow,
the tiger lily's shape a lost embrace, just out of reach.
Then deep within the tone of hollow days
Gabriel's wings unfurl, slicing emptiness into ribbons of light,
love's unflinching gaze hot as summer sun.

JOANIE HIEGER FRITZ ZOSIKE

"S" Is for "Summer"

I remember summer
As sand, salt, sea,
Sweat, sex, sensibility
Sensuously straddling
Sweet supine succulent
Boy flesh, severely
Shaken by shivers of
Satisfaction

Summer was a temptress
Tantalizing me, a moment to
Seek a source of sixpence, find
The serpentine meat of time
The rhythm of another year
Spent falling crosswise with intent
To bisect the spine of the
Sundial

In the sunshine with the
Sunflowers and sweet aspidistra,
Swollen berries and sizzling skin
Overstayed moments in the sun,
We'd run through the showers of
Priapic heat held stoically back till it
Squeezed through smoky tumescent
Clouds

Released in sun showers, surprising
Concertgoers on a sumptuous lawn
Slushing, slanting, pelting rain chasing
The music, soaking the picnic, ruining
Sandals, lacy socks and silky summer
Frocks, startling laughing cherubs,
We'd slyly shimmy back to straw mat
Rooms

Tips of tongues meet quivering legs
Emerge from the brine of the sea,
Crustaceans of old resurface anew
Everything underfoot burns grey
Fades away and dries; the succubus sky
Has gone, the sloop is empty, no one
Sails anymore, we've reached autumn's
Door

KENDALL STEINLE

Ardent

At noon, a full week after the tire factory went up in flames, the sky was *still* orange. And the air *still* smelled like smoke. People lost jobs and kids lost parents, but that's all I could think about. The orange. The smoke.

We were taking a walk, a week before I was to jump the pond. We had had the best summer: no flags or holy books were torched that summer—just those tires.

That summer, I had made him laugh. I had made him cry, made him fall in love with me, made him doubt his very existence, made him irate and made his body numb, but I could rarely make the kid laugh. But that summer, I did. People cried and people died and there we were, just the two of us, in the orange and in the smoke, and I had made him laugh.

We both saw it at the same time—a wad of bills on the ground. We stood over it, silent, forever. It was a trick. It had to be.

We looked around. The mansions did not look back.

He picked it up, held it high in the air, waiting for the owner to claim it.

"Did somebody drop this?" he called.

He flipped the greenbacks over to see if any strings were attached, our glances around the neighborhood jerky and quick and crack-like. We rode a most unnatural and rigid gait back home to my front porch and smashed the bank wide open.

He said he wanted to donate it to the *masjid*, I said to a local animal shelter. He said to give it to my dad to be nice (to make amends). I said to buy his mother flowers (to make amends). I told him to keep it, he told me to keep it, he saw it first, I saw it first, he said he'd give me anything (update: this turned out to be a lie).

Paul said anything over fifty bucks should be turned in, so we lied and said it was forty-nine, donated nothing, bought gas, bought dinner, thought about buying condoms but didn't and should have, like really should have, but we had enough to buy something to save our backs, bought movie tickets and paid some people back, thought about paying some other people back and then thought better of it, bought some flashlights for future walks, but of course we never took another walk, because I left and he left and I don't know what happened to the rest of the money, or him, or the kid that lost his dad in a torrid fireball of smoldering rubber but I'm telling you, the sky is still orange and it still smells like smoke and it was the best summer we'd ever had.

ELLARAINE LOCKIE

After Montana

The guys in the California coffee shop
say I look like I've been with a new lover
I could tell them how wind
slides over skin like a feather duster
How the silk of knee-deep grass strokes bare legs
The face tickle of a spider strand on a sigh of air
That wears the pale perfume
of yellow prairie clover in full bloom
And hollyhocks stand higher and straighter
than any man you've been with
Stubble like an unshaved man with Clint Eastwood legs
Beneath it all a bed of rich soil
on which you've longed to lie for the past year

I could tell them how annual equals cutting-edge new
When wind licks with different tongues each time
Runs a reborn hand over your hills and gullies
And a bee with black lingerie wings humps the blossom
of a Canadian thistle that wasn't there yesterday
How July's breath exhales hotter with each hour
How when it rises and lifts a skirt
it can make a woman wet long before raindrops

Until her entire body is sweat slippery
Thunder moans in the deep throat of distance
And you try to think of something besides S&M
to justify the thrill of wild rose thorns brushing your legs
The sound of a screen slapping the air
Pulsing of power lines and tumbleweeds
that dirty dance until the whole prairie swells

I could tell the guys how the hands of wind
shake a tree trunk until it's stripped of leaves
And cottonwood branches bend in evocative positions
That when hail hits like popcorn frying in a pan
butter melts and drips in a cabin

➤

How afterward trains whoop
Pussywillows and cattails hang limp and still
Afterglow flickers like the twilight of a candle
And sunflowers stare through their brown voyeur eyes
under a sky that blushes salmon, rust and rose

But instead I just say how Montana men call me *Kiddo*
See the 15-year-old girl who tried
to get the air changed in her Chevy's tires
And the California guys return to whatever tall tales
men tell each other in coffee shops

First published in *Schuykill Valley Journal*

PHILIP VERMAAS

Object Desire

Inwear, Outwear, Herewear, Starewear, Theirwear, Wearhouse, Wearhoes, Whocareswear,

whatever the boutique
for slim, hip,
not hippy,
nor hippie,
young urban women
is called.

That you can shop here,
is not the thing;
it's the slim, hip,
not hippy,
nor hippie,
mannequins:
a lot of them,
too many of them,
a front-line dozen,
in flimsy summer-fashion fatigues,
on pedestals
towering over me,
staring into the distance;
eyes in sunglasses
on heads cocked up
to an unnatural degree:
the angle of aspired-to contempt.

Except the last one,
crouching
and, without sunglasses,
looking askance,
in the opposite direction
of her Titan sisters seeking
utopian sun.
Maybe she's
the concrete-jungle hunter at midnight,
maybe she's just their bitch.
If she was only still to be removed,
it doesn't matter,
she's the one about which
I had the dirty thought.

First published in *Better Cigarettes and Other Poems* (Blue Hour Press, 2013)

ANTON CHEKHOV

At a Summer Villa

"I love you. You are my life, my happiness—everything to me! Forgive the avowal, but I have not the strength to suffer and be silent. I ask not for love in return, but for sympathy. Be at the old arbor at eight o'clock this evening. To sign my name is unnecessary I think, but do not be uneasy at my being anonymous. I am young, nice-looking… what more do you want?"

When Pavel Ivanitch Vyhodtsev, a practical married man who was spending his holidays at a summer villa, read this letter, he shrugged his shoulders and scratched his forehead in perplexity.

"What devilry is this?" he thought. "I'm a married man, and to send me such a queer, silly letter! Who wrote it?"

Pavel Ivanitch turned the letter over and over before his eyes, read it through again, and spat with disgust.

"'I love you,'" he said jeeringly. "A nice boy she has pitched on! So I'm to run off to meet you in the arbor! I got over all such romances and *fleurs d'amour* years ago, my girl. Hmm! She must be some reckless, immoral creature. Well, these women are a set! What a whirligig—God forgive us!—she must be to write a letter like that to a stranger, and a married man, too! It's real demoralization!"

In the course of his eight years of married life, Pavel Ivanitch had completely got over all sentimental feeling, and he had received no letters from ladies except letters of congratulation, and so, although he tried to carry it off with disdain, the letter quoted above greatly intrigued and agitated him.

An hour after receiving it, he was lying on his sofa, thinking: "Of course I am not a silly boy, and I am not going to rush off to this idiotic rendezvous; but yet it would be interesting to know who wrote it! Hmm. It is certainly a woman's writing. The letter is written with genuine feeling, and so it can hardly be a joke. Most likely it's some neurotic girl, or perhaps a widow…widows are frivolous and eccentric as a rule. Hmm…Who could it be?"

What made it the more difficult to decide the question was that Pavel Ivanitch had not one feminine acquaintance among all the summer visitors, except his wife.

"It is queer," he mused. "'I love you!'…When did she manage to fall in love? Amazing woman! To fall in love like this, apropos of nothing, without making any acquaintance and finding out what sort of man I am…She must be extremely young and romantic if she is capable of falling in love after two or three looks at me…But…who is she?"

Pavel Ivanitch suddenly recalled that when he had been walking among the summer villas the day before, and the day before that, he had several times been met by a fair young lady with a light blue hat and a turned-up nose. The fair charmer had kept looking at him, and when he sat down on a seat she had sat down beside him.

"Can it be she?" he wondered. "It can't be! Could a delicate ephemeral creature like that fall in love with a worn-out old eel like me? No, it's impossible!"

At dinner, Pavel Ivanitch looked blankly at his wife while he meditated:

"She writes that she is young and nice-looking…So she's not old…Hmm…To tell the truth, honestly, I am not so old and plain that no one could fall in love with me. My wife loves me! Besides, love is blind, we all know."

"What are you thinking about?" his wife asked him.

"Oh…my head aches a little," Pavel Ivanitch said, quite untruly.

He made up his mind that it was stupid to pay attention to such a nonsensical thing as a love letter and laughed at it and at its authoress. After dinner, Pavel Ivanitch lay down on his bed and instead of going to sleep, reflected:

"But there, I daresay she is expecting me to come! What a silly! I can just imagine what a nervous fidget she'll be in when she does not find me in the arbor! I shan't go." But a half hour later he was musing, "Perhaps I might go just out of curiosity…I might go and look from a distance what sort of a creature she is. It would be interesting to have a look at her! It would be fun, and that's all! After all, why shouldn't I have a little fun since such a chance has turned up?"

Pavel Ivanitch got up from his bed and began dressing. "What are you getting yourself up so smartly for?" his wife asked, noticing that he was putting on a clean shirt and a fashionable tie.

"Oh, nothing. I must have a walk. My head aches."

Pavel Ivanitch dressed in his best, and, waiting till eight o'clock, went out of the house. When the figures of gaily dressed summer visitors of both sexes began passing before his eyes against the bright green background, his heart throbbed.

"Which of them is it?" he wondered, advancing irresolutely. "Come, what am I afraid of? Why, I am not going to the rendezvous! What a fool! Go forward boldly! And what if I go into the arbor? Well, well…there is no reason I should."

Pavel Ivanitch's heart beat still more violently…Involuntarily, with no desire to do so, he suddenly pictured to himself the half-darkness of the arbor. A graceful fair girl with a little blue hat and a turned-up nose rose before his imagination. He saw her, abashed by her love and trembling all over, timidly approach him, breathing excitedly, and…suddenly clasping him in her arms.

"If I weren't married it would be all right, " he mused, driving sinful ideas out of his head. "Though…for once in my life, it would do no harm to have the experience, or else one will die without knowing what…And my wife, what will it matter to her? Thank God, for eight years I've never moved one step away from her…Eight years of irreproachable duty! Enough of her. It's positively vexatious. I'm ready to go to spite her!"

Trembling all over and holding his breath, Pavel Ivanitch went up to the arbor, wreathed with ivy and wild vine, and peeped into it…A smell of dampness and mildew reached him.

"I believe there's nobody…" he thought, going into the arbor, and at once saw a human silhouette in the corner.

The silhouette was that of a man….Looking more closely, Pavel Ivanitch recognized his wife's brother, Mitya, a student, who was staying with them at the villa.

"Oh, it's you…" he growled discontentedly, as he took off his hat and sat down.

"Yes, it's I," answered Mitya.

Two minutes passed in silence.

"Excuse me, Pavel Ivanitch," began Mitya, "but might I ask you to leave me alone? I am thinking over the dissertation for my degree and the presence of anybody else prevents my thinking."

"You had better go somewhere in a dark avenue," Pavel Ivanitch observed mildly. "It's easier to think in the open air, and, besides, I should like to have a little sleep here on this seat. It's not so hot here."

"You want to sleep, but it's a question of my dissertation," Mitya grumbled. "The dissertation is more important."

Again there was a silence. Pavel Ivanitch, who had given the rein to his imagination and was continually hearing footsteps, suddenly leaped up and said in a plaintive voice:

"Come, I beg you, Mitya! You are younger and ought to consider me . I am unwell and I need sleep. Go away!"

"That's egoism. Why must you be here and not I? I won't go as a matter of principle."

"Come, I ask you to! Suppose I am an egoist, a despot and a fool…but I ask you to go! For once in my life I ask you a favor! Show some consideration!"

Mitya shook his head.

"What a beast!" thought Pavel Ivanitch. "That can't be a rendezvous with him here! It's impossible with him here!"

"I say, Mitya," he said, "I ask you for the last time. Show that you are a sensible, humane, and cultivated man!"

"I don't know why you keep on so!" said Mitya, shrugging his shoulders. "I've said I won't go, and I won't. I shall stay here as a matter of principle."

At that moment, a woman's face with a turned-up nose peeped into the arbor.

Seeing Mitya and Pavel Ivanitch, it frowned and vanished.

"She is gone!" thought Pavel Ivanitch, looking angrily at Mitya. She saw that blackguard and fled! It's all spoilt!

After waiting a little longer, he got up, put on his hat, and said:

"You're a beast, a low brute and a blackguard! Yes! A beast! It's mean and silly! Everything is at an end between us!"

"Delighted to hear it!" muttered Mitya, also getting up and putting on his hat. "Let me tell you that by being here just now you've played me such a dirty trick that I'll never forgive you as long as I live."

Pavel Ivanitch went out of the arbor, and beside himself with rage, strode rapidly to his villa. Even the sight of the table laid for supper did not soothe him.

"Once in a lifetime such a chance has turned up," he thought in agitation, "and then it's been prevented! Now she is offended, crushed!"

At supper, Pavel Ivanitch and Mitya kept their eyes on their plates and maintained a sullen silence. They were hating each other from the bottom of their hearts.

"What are you smiling at?" asked Pavel Ivanitch, pouncing on his wife. "It's only silly fools who laugh for nothing!"

His wife looked at her husband's angry face, and went off into a peal of laughter.

"What was that letter you got this morning?" she asked.

"I…I didn't get one." Pavel Ivanitch was overcome with confusion. "You are inventing…imagination."

"Oh, come, tell us! Own up, you did! Why, it was I sent you that letter! Honor bright, I did! Ha ha!"

Pavel Ivanitch turned crimson and bent over his plate. "Silly jokes," he growled.

"But what could I do? Tell me that. We had to scrub the rooms out this evening, and how could we get you out of the house? There was no other way of getting you out. But don't be angry, stupid. I didn't want you to be dull in the arbor, so I sent the same letter to Mitya too! Mitya, have you been to the arbor?"

Mitya grinned and left off glaring with hatred at his rival.

Translated by Constance Garnett

PAUL NEBENZAHL

Here's to the Singer of Songs

Here's to the singer of songs
The siren of adventure
Who crept into my chest cavity a few nights ago
When it was hot, ghastly so, and the tepee room
Dripped with its own cedar sweat

For I was thinking of tearing at my skin
When I had shed my clothes
The cool bath hardly helped
I paced nude from back to front
Looking for a break in the weather

The dogs, as well, mesmerized by the heat
Laid on cool wood floors and sped up their breath
To cool their pulses, I had half a mind to shave them
Their regal coats it has been explained to me
Served to keep them at an even keel in all types of climes

Thinking about my Mother, who had come from Peru, Illinois
And grew up in hot, dusty Moline
Her stories of her first year in Chicago
A bohemian summer where poets and their drinking readers
Slept on Fullerton Beach, on fire escapes and rooftops

And remembering my Dad, his early jungle flesh
Was the wonder of Senn High, a gay tenor
He too had talked about things he did
To stay cool when the miles of pavement were burning
Holding the hot sun long after it had passed the coast out west

I was in a tizzy
I imagined the grim reaper was just outside the door
With a hot poker to stick into me again and again
My reading in the bath had been leaning to the thirties
And the forties when men and women burned dead or alive in ovens

You might say I was off the program that night
My darling tucked in seven states away too late to call

➤

The one air device I hooked up to the window and the outlet
Hardly made a dent in the blast
So intense was the furnace that stayed burning long after sunset

Relief, which will often come from the horn of Miles Davis
I play Miles into the night some evenings seeking solace
His long lines stretching out like lanterns on the water
Being pushed by a gentle breeze
His sense of strategy a balm for worry and an open door of wonder

But that night Miles didn't click
Nor did Coleman Hawkins, or Muddy Waters
My old standby saints of sound
Heard them crooked not straight
And put away, finally, the sounds that often calm

Same with television, it made the room hotter
The story lines hard to follow
What was I in the mood for?
Mystery, drama, romance
Closed the computer screen down, and ran ice along my face

Sonny heard it first
A crack of thunder split the sky at two o'clock a.m.
And then the heavens simply opened up
I was transported back to earlier summer nights
When we ran in the rain in the nude in our big backyard

And then both dogs were howling
The thunder chasing lightning, just seconds apart
We could see the street bright as day, brighter
When the lightning struck down the block
And the rain pounded on the roof over our heads

Quiet like, without discussion
The kind that a man sometimes has with his dogs
We lit down the back stairs to see the night storm
And feel the air to find out its nature, we knew
Going down or going up, it was just going

Without a leash we opened the fence gate, and walked to the street
Dogs and I, we let the cool rain soak us
Soon drenched with cool water, hair matted and clothes soaked

The dogs walked right next to me, without a sound
Without a command needed to keep them close

We walked for a hour, the power now snapped out
The whole neighborhood dark as coal
One house at Ashland and Wilder had candles in the window
I could hear the last drinks being poured at the rain party
Inside that hot little house on the corner

I was laughing, low and deep
A belly laugh from way inside
At the turn of events and the pounding rain
It must have dropped thirty degrees
From one hundred to seventy in five minutes flat

My dogs on either side of me
Understanding that this needed to be
They trudged along touching my wet legs
And looking up at me
I swear they were both smiling in the pouring rain.

ante meridiem III *dear "how-silently-the-heart-pivots-on-its-hinges,"*

i have a shrapnel desire for vagueness
because nearness is more than a shared
windshield worldview, because nearness
questions the practice of ellipses—spotlights
exclamation marks' truancy—makes a wish,
but nearness colors daruma's wrong eye,
then proclaims that russian dolls
 are so full of themselves

i have a shrapnel desire
 for vagueness, there's no
 such thing as direct
communication—only faint
spiderwebs—tethering
 the densities of yeast and
breaths of pith—people
don't listen, they wait for their turn to talk,
unsolicited adornment

i have a shrapnel
desire for vagueness
because clarity is
perishable—porous,
deeper than horse
piss on
murk
 snow

your one and only,
nearsighted loner

JAX NTP

ante meridiem VIII *savoring the butterscotch intervals between seconds of non-sextions*

my belly is an old dryer, your touch, an even older pair of grey vans,
thump. thump. when you draw lines of suspension on my hungry-is-not-

a-strong-enough-word-this-skin, is it more or less suggestive to tessellating frayed nerves?
e-late. illicitations. your top lip arch is a heron mid-wing-flap,

shawling tripwires of potential. to unpack our eager fancy now would be
clumsy, pedestrian. i am a mullet, fawning for symmetry, at best, waiting for the jump.

the inflections in your sighs cut off at just the ripe angle of 83 degrees, slanting unto me,
into me, thicker than calligraphy, more percolating than pulmonaria.

i'm not the initial soot, but leftover soot on side furnaces of brick buildings.
your body, three quarters of a summer's night, i could sleep in the cold of you

JAX NTP

ante meridiem X *prose-stitute*

the nape of your neck, more buttery than avocado saturated
in extra-virgin olive-oil. clay flakes. wolf crepes. frustascular
8-0-8. detonations to your thighs. step your watch and gap

the mind. don't hesitate—fumble, fumble thru the flood.
would you say an observer is an absorber? tell me more
about osmosis and filters. cyan pigments absorb the most

red light. there are so many grains precisely halfway between
that blue and this green, more grainy than undercooked mushroom
risotto. runny custard. sprawling iotas of potential—butterscotch

tendrils drip into the phrases of us. here, hippety-hop
synchronicity. epi-curious drollic, whisk, whisked. our
flautist duet, my oracle to your omen, the trumpets

glow again. our bones suspended in the alphabet
you braided my aureolas with your marmalade. fingering
sicilianas—let my fig leaf tambour through your sonata.

jussulent tandem, juicy sinew. emit omissions. i type a few
words, halfhearted percolations. delete half of them, no,
delete all of them. reach out for a cigarette that is not there

because i don't smoke. reach out for your hands, but you're
 not here—because you're not here, and in this moment, pregnant
 thoughts yield mimeographic re-discoveries of misplaced

equilibriums. mind my gaps and watch your steps.
 i find myself, content, finally, with stillness, unmarred
by somnambulism. tessellated nebulas thrust

into impermeable soil. i left my galaxy
charger in your purse. you kept my
galaxy with your curse. when breasts

 of stones heave
open, rushed.
rush

---

eating light

We take breakfast on the lawn:
raw tuna, rice and beer.
The sun is warmer than usual.
You sit cross-legged in the heat.
I am looking up your kimono.
The light is right.

THOMAS KUDLA

The Summer's Maddest of Loves

I was in bed with my past. She kindly reminded me of why I moved on and had a completely different girl in my bed the night before. My past – she moved my hand where she dreamt it to be, where her church warned her it might be. And she told me to stop. She braced my lips for a trembling tease of the tongue, and I moved with the waves of the innocence lost quivering in her hazelnut eyes. We were moving in natural motions most like rhythm—and then she told me to stop. Again and again this passive aggression of my past led me to remember the day before, when I was cradling a gifted young woman with stars in her eyes, reminding me of the summer's maddest of loves, written across my skin.

My past saw the tattoo on my right bicep. She traced it gently with her softened fingers as if she knew how sacred it was, how sacred it had become, how sacred it would always be. This—the symbol of her savior twisted into a gothic immortality—this would keep my past from knowing my future. We never made love that night. We never made love any night. And this perhaps is why she is my past.

The night before was full of wonder. She was the only star in the sky. She came down to lighten my heart just enough as to worry my past. It's no wonder that my confessions weren't confessions—I never cheated; I just played more often. They both didn't need to become rivals—they knew they shared a resigned jealousy, and a common competition for my attention and affection. The past knew what she was. And the star saw deep enough into my heart to know of the summer's maddest of loves, that which I will never forget, that which told its story across my skin.

Hope disguised herself in a gorgeous love at first sight that summer. She wore punk rock like a diamond ring and heavy metal like a rosary. Hail Mary, full of grace, scream your beauty into my belly. When she sang about love, she danced to the heartbeats of revolution. Blessed art thou who find love in poetry, photography, and deathly imagery. She brushed her hair in rainbows, just because she knew most everyone only pretends they're color blind. Holy Mary, mother of rock gods, break the strings on our guitars with the passion we thought we lost. She looked to the sky from the mosh pit.

The summer's maddest of loves stares at me in the mirror each morning. Some days I look away. I don't want to believe in love. Other days I trace it with my fingertips. Why'd it have to stop? Its red infinity sign holds an imaginary savior's arms like wings. Fly away to Heaven, and there's always hope. Hope will look at me from that crucifix on my arm even if I ignore her. She's as much a part of me now as my heart itself.

The summer's maddest of loves hopes I look at her grace and meaning not out of appreciation, but out of reminiscence. She drew herself from my heart onto the bloodied canvas of my tattooed bicep. The red of the infinity sign is borne from my heart. The summer's maddest of loves knows this and will keep reminding me until her hope becomes reality.

❖

That summer I was recovering from a break with my past. I was still clinging on, trying to convince her and me that we had a future together. But the past, oh, the past—she is named as such because we have no future together. Then an unexpected spark ignited an amnesia of an aphrodisiac. You see, I was reunited with this girl I'd known since teen years, but we never knew each other—really knew each other, that is, until she transformed herself into hope—the summer's maddest of loves.

For some odd reason, when I showed up at a stranger's house that brilliant day, that day when the sun reflected itself off every step with a frenetic charm, hope ran to me for a huge hug. We hadn't seen each other for quite some time. Seeing as how she was quite possibly the only person I knew at the stranger's house, I intensified the hug—a lift and a twist side to side. This warmest of hugs served as foreshadowing of the summer's maddest of loves. Our eyes met perfectly still and pupil to pupil, our arms and shoulders interlocked like lovers' lips, and our bodies floated together as two intertwined party balloons tied down only by gravity. It would remain this way the entire evening, and the rest of the summer, with our minds only strengthening what we already felt, what we already knew.

We took a long way home from a drive-in theater. I parked in her driveway. She rested her head in my lap as I read my poetry to her.

"When I say I'm in love/the meaning is/meaning."

This went on until six in the morn. Just before daybreak she asked me if she could kiss me. I answered with a turn of my head and a leaning downward. She looked up so adoringly and so confidently. I don't know if it was the blood rushing to my brain from leaning down like that, which caused a bit of lightheadedness as we kissed, but I like to think it was a rare form of love—the summer's maddest of loves.

Every day with her was another reason to wake up early. Every night with her was another reason to stay up late. She was a lover. She was a best friend. She was a muse. When I wasn't spending time with her, I was writing poetry inspired by her. I was afflicted with a bliss I hadn't felt often before. This feverish love was a hopeful kind of love, a love to enjoy life with, a love to run with, a love to make, a love to cherish forever, a love to be reminded of by inked skin—it was the summer's maddest of loves.

We shared our friends like ideas and good times. During the day, as I drove from my friend's place to her friend's place, from restaurant to pool hall, from here to there, the soundtrack would continue. With the windows down and the sun shining bright from above, her hands would flutter like butterflies with the breeze. She'd sing to the music she had picked for our short road trip adventures.

"I'm free, free-fallin.'"

"This song is us," she told me.

And now, every time I hear that song, I think of she and I, and the free-fallin' and the free-lovin' and the flyin' and the breathin' and the dreamin' and the dancin' and the summer's maddest of loves.

Another time, we were listening to a punk-rock song about how everyone you meet leaves a mark on your soul. I was determined that the mark she would leave on my soul would be beautiful beyond compare.

I respected her art so much. I asked her to create a tattoo for me, one based on a concept I had been thinking about for quite some time. Back then, the tattoo was meant to be a symbol of the eternal pursuit of divinity—a crucifix with an infinity sign in place of a horizontal bar. By having her create it, I had altered its meaning. Often I look at that symbol now and see the eternal pursuit of love. Is there any difference?

The moment I saw it, I loved it. She went with black and red, the infinity sign being of the latter color. Whereas the crucifixion was deathly dark, the divinity-now-rendered-lovely was alive and blood red.

I was driving to the tattoo parlor with her. She rested her head on my lap as I drove. A rainstorm touched down upon the dark veil of night. The rain poured. Thunderbolts jolted through our seats. She didn't move much at all. She said rain was soothing to her. And then I asked her if it's the same with lightning. At that moment a lightning bolt seemed to strike the grass not many yards in front of us off the side of the road. This got her attention. I was as excited about it as she was scared.

At the parlor, I brought in the design she had created for me. The tattoo artist, whose rock star dreams had led to this parlor, began setting up after he traced the design. He tried his best to make small talk.

"We do this because we're laughing at death," he said, reaching for the needle.

"I don't know, man, I think life is pretty fuckin' funny." I laughed uproariously, but he didn't think it was that funny. I thought I knew so much. And he knew I didn't know anything. I was mad. But that didn't matter, because she was there with me as I would be forever marked.

She asked me what it felt like as the artist worked at his craft. I wasn't looking at my bicep, but she told me it was bleeding like crazy. All I could see was that lightning bolt from our car drive. It was touching down on my skin instead of the horizon.

"A bunch of thunderbolts."

She grabbed my hand and held it tightly as if afraid for me.

"It's the greatest feeling."

Afterward, we went to my friend's apartment. I showed off the tattoo. I began discussing my plans for seven piercings and an extreme change in hair color.

"Let's get a photo of you before you do all that," my friend said, scavenging for his camera. "You know, a before-and-after thing."

I agreed, but then I came up with this idea. I told the summer's maddest of loves to stand with me, back-to-back, arms interlocked. I told her to do whatever she wanted with her body and I would do the same. We wouldn't talk to one another about it. We would just see the end result. My friend didn't describe it. He said we'd have to look for ourselves when the photos got developed.

Back at college, I received the photos in the mail. I was already distancing myself from my past and constantly reminding myself of the summer's maddest of loves. I didn't know with certainty why my past and I had lacked chemistry as of late. Then I saw that photo, and it all became clear.

She held her palms open and her head lifted, her eyes glistening with hopeful anticipation for future blessings from above; I held my hands closed into fists and my head downward almost to my neck, my eyes drifting shut, weary from a life well-lived. The whole of me and the whole of she complemented each other so perfectly.

As perfect as we were together, it was only for that moment in time, for that mad summer. She and I eventually lost touch. Somehow our busy lives and the state borders between us created barriers that couldn't be transcended. Yet I look in that mirror, I see the lightning flash, I touch my arm, I feel the needle's thunderbolts—and I remember her. I remember the way we hugged. The beautiful rebellion. The blessed freedom. The arms interlocked. The photo. The music. How she asked to kiss me. How I didn't need to say anything. Hands dancing with the breeze. Car free-fallin' down the hills. Laughing at death because life isn't funny enough. I remember all of these things. I remember her. And I know there's hope for a love this true. I may never see her again, but at least she left her mark on my soul—a tattoo representing the summer's maddest of loves.

First published in *What My Brain Told Me,* a collection of short stories by Thomas Kudla (Lulu, 2008)

JERI THOMPSON

Summer Romance
      for Frank

I can't have sex like a man
Anymore. It takes too much
Time to unravel the knots in my head
And my back (after our recent skirmishes).
I need to giggle with you over morning coffee and kiss
Your midnight worries away and curl up in
Your strong arms…those strong arms.

I need a soft place to land, not just
Sweating, groaning, wrestling—
Us, embattled in a separate quest;
Impersonal, intense, impenetrable.
We battle alone while I want
To build a community of two
That reaches across
Many summers.

Thank you for reminding me
That winter has not arrived
For me,
Yet.

JERI THOMPSON

His Smile

As I pass him on his corner, a week after our mutual break-up
(Still friends, just in different places),
He smiles, and it speaks to me:
It says "We have a secret, no one will know"
It says, "I remember you in my bed."
It says, "I can still taste your pleasure."
His smile would have brought me to my knees
Any other day. Today, as I remember him—
His smooth caramel skin, the scent of his soap, his guttural tones—
I also remember his heart,
Something I will never possess
Although I want it still.
I manage a return smile:
As my knees hold up,
As I keep walking forward,
Towards the waning summer sun.

DONNA HILBERT

Neophyte and the Swan

He shattered her glass
climbing over the table
to kiss her, that hot afternoon,
when she quoted his poem over wine.
It was free verse, abstract in part,
and difficult, he knew,
committing it to heart.
They kissed the afternoon away,
and on the drive back, kissed
through every stop sign and red light.
Between the kisses
he smoked a cigarette.
And, what she failed to reconcile
about that day, was the casual way
he tossed the ember from the window,
considering how hot and dry the summer,
how much fuel there was to burn.

First published in *The Congress of Luminous Bodies* (Aortic Books, 2013)

RUTH MOON KEMPHER

Hot Dog Stand Drama

She, whispering: How long has it been?
   (clutches frosty bottles against her blouse)
   Is it three years now? Or four? Or even five?
He (trying not to laugh, or cry): It's about four.
    It's about time to re-up. Re-enlist. Something.
   (also watches the bottles, as they slip in her arms)
She: Isn't that crazy. I should have remembered.
He, nodding: No reason you should have.
     Watch it....you're dropping those bottles.
She (her smile is sudden): You know I almost said
    I've got to go, before these drinks get cold.
    (Her voice falters.) What I meant was...
He, careful, polite: Sure. I know. It was
     sure nice, seeing you again. (Watches her legs
     make scissor shadows across the sand.)
The Vendor: Hey. (His eyes glitter
     dark in the background.) You know that chick?
     Know her a lot, I'd bet.
He, leaning on the counter, counting the packages
     in the wire stand: seven chocolate, nine
     peanut butter: Just a little.
     And it was a long time ago. And we were never
     even introduced. Not officially. We just
     saw each other, and danced a little.
     Like now. It doesn't matter.
The Vendor, swiping at the counter; his
     rag splatters: That don't make sense to me
     But listen, Bud, you come here for something
     so what is it? A dog? A beer? Got good mustard
     burns your gut. Straight from It'ly.
A Breeze, enters. Takes the Vendor's suggestions
     and flings them surfward, where they fold in
     joining minnows, bottle bits, old
     shell shards. Whirls away.

First published in *Old Red Kimono*

Porgy Agonistes

Slouching from Birdland to be reborn
with Nina's *Loves You, Porgy*
flowing in a marquee chord,
I was accosted
by the shade of Sporting Life,
slick as sin and high as happy dust,
He taunted, "Lookin' for a girl, son?"
and vanished down a subway.

Then I was struck blind
by the apocalypse of Porgy,
whipping his goat along a desolate White Way,
uprooting skyscrapers like abscessed molars,
leveling, with the arm that crushed hot Crown,
the whole sophisticated, pimping facade.
"Where is you, Bess? Where is you?"

That is the parable
of black romanticism,
the moral Armageddon
of a goat cart and a strong right arm.

EDNA ST. VINCENT MILLAY

Summer Sonnet

I know I am but summer to your heart,
And not the full four seasons of the year;
And you must welcome from another part
Such noble moods as are not mine, my dear.
No gracious weight of golden fruits to sell
Have I, nor any wise and wintry thing;
And I have loved you all too long and well
To carry still the high sweet breast of spring.
Wherefore I say: O love, as summer goes,
I must be gone, steal forth with silent drums,
That you may hail anew the bird and rose
When I come back to you, as summer comes.
Else will you seek, at some not distant time,
Even your summer in another clime.

Empty Hours
        For Marlain

i want you
barefoot
knocked up
in the kitchen
singing
all your favorite
love songs, watching
summer skies
circle overhead.

i want you
asleep
on the bed
with a book left
open somewhere
nearby. i want you

in the cold empty hours,
when the lights
go out, and only
the memory
of you here with me,
remains.

i want you
in the kitchen
humming
while your hands
wrinkle
in hot dish soap
water. i want you

here holding our child
within the grasp
of your hips,
and your breath
to become the sweet
lullaby i sleep to,

and wake
to find you
singing
in the kitchen.

PART V
AQUA

Summer Celestial

At dusk I row out to what looks like light or anonymity,
too far from land to be called to, too close to be lost,
and drag oar until I can drift in and out of a circle,
the center of a circle, nothing named, nothing now to see,
the wind up a little and down, building against the air,
and listen to anything at all, bird or wind, or nothing
but the first sounds on the surface, clarifying, clear.

Once, in Canada, I saw a man stand up in his boat and pass
out dollar bills. It was summer dark. They blew down
on the lake like moonlight. Coming out of his hands
they looked like dollar bills. When I look up at the Dippers,
the whole star chart, leaves on a tree, sometimes all night,
I think about his balance over cold water, under stars,
standing in a shoe, the nets all down and gathering.

My mother still wakes crying do I think she's made of money
—And what makes money make money make money?
I wish I could tell her how to talk herself to sleep.
I wish. She says she's afraid she won't make it back.
As in a prayer, she is more afraid of loneliness than death.
Two pennies for eyes, two cents: I wish I could tell her
that each day the stars reorganize, each night they come back new.

Outside tonight the waters run to color with the sky.
In the old water dream you wake up in a boat, drifting out.
Everything is cold and smells of rain. Somewhere back there,
in sleep, you remember weeping. And at this moment you think.
you are about to speak. But someone is holding on, hand
over hand, and someone with your voice opening and closing.
In water you think it will always be your face that floats

to the surface. Flesh is on fire under water. The nets go back
to gather and regather, and bring up stones, viridian and silver,
what falls. In the story, the three Dutch fishermen sail out
for stars, into the daylight hours, so loaded with their catch
it spills. They sleep, believe it, where they can, and dry
their nets on a full moon. For my mother, who is afraid to sleep,
for anyone afraid of heights or water, all of this is intolerable.

Look, said the wish, into your lover's face. Mine over yours.
In that other life, which I now commend to you, I have spent
the days by a house along the shore, building a boat, tying
the nets together, watching the lights go on and off on the water.
But nothing gets gone, none of it ever gets finished. So I lie down
in a dream of money being passed from hand to hand in a long line.
It looks like money—or hands taking hands, being led out

to deeper water. I wake up weeping, and it is almost joy.
I go outside and the sky is sea-blue, the way the earth is looked at
from the moon. And out on the great surfaces, water is paying
back water. I know. I know this is a day and the stars reiterate,
return each loss, each witness. And that always in the rooms next door
someone is coughing all night or a man and a woman make love.
each body buoyed, even blessed, by what the other cannot have.

From *Summer Celestial* (The Ecco Press, NY, 1983)

RICK SMITH

Rafting On The Kern River (7/07)

ride the Kern River
in late July,
feel the broad shaft of heat
and, in shadow,
beneath an expanse of bridge
carrying trucks from Bakersfield,
the grid hums;
you can hear it
over the rush and roar.

a man my age
may fall out of a raft
at a hairpin turn
innocently named
"Deadman's Curve,"
a foot wedged against rock,
toe to toe with the stony bed,
eyes only inches from the foam of surface
and pinned by current,
he holds a final burning breath,
expects to rise,
he sees light through air pockets.

sometimes a river raft
may climb onto a boulder
for no reason at noon
while a family orders shrimp scampi
at an outdoor grill in town.

ride the river as it swells
and makes its way
gargling and spitting us out
in an instant
like mouth wash.

the sound of a helicopter
takes another millennium
to arrive.

Gone Fishing

i remember
looking at the worms
lying in the
cool
moist
soil
even though
they weren't
below my feet
below the grass
they seemed
at home
in the white
styrofoam
cup
nothing was
really
out of place
until i sent
the steel barbed hook i held
through them
the movement of a worm
on a hook
should make you
sleepless
forever
i then cast
death
into the
black water
and waited for my
red and white
bobber
to bring me
more

DIRK VELVET

School Car Wash

those
poor
artless
lambs
holding signs
in
tank tops
and
shorts
calling in
those men
with their cars
already
clean

RUTH MOON KEMPHER

On the Beach, Hot

prowleyed women
greased for the ceremonials
upelbow at high noon's approach—
      here's a child priest, with shovel
crouched, ready—
as leathery old apostles castle in the sand.

      First published in *Ale House*

SUSIE SWEETLAND GARAY

Where the Grass and Light Meet

There is this place
at the beach in a
sort of sand dune
valley where you are
one crest away from
your first glorious view
and the grass and the
light meet and mix
perfectly.

Things are always
breaking down,
but happiness is
not something to
be sneered at.

I try to quantify,
but the dirt under
my fingernails only
stares back at me,
unresponsive.

It is not a tragedy.

You point at the
Harriers as they
do their dance.
He circles, showing
off, flying in patterns,
as she follows.
We drink our
drinks and watch
the sun go down.

I walk into a room
that is filled
with something
I can't breathe.

Self-talk works to
calm me, but I am
getting tired of
my own repetitions.

win harms

if it were a summer rain
it would feel cool
upon my face
refreshing
i would welcome it
gratefully
i'd dance among the
raindrops
thankful for the
sudden drop in temperature
if it was a summer rain
i'd climb into his bed and heart
he would hold me until it ended
then we would go to get ice cream
or some other summer thing
but this is not a summer rain
this is mid December
cold and cruel
it keeps me banished
to my room
dreaming of his touch
and sweet memories
of summer rain

DANIEL McGINN

after a dry season

it's the twist
of your tongue
in my mouth
the words you whisper
in my lungs
that make me
make noise
make that noise
that warm breath
blue as air
and twice as green

my name still hangs
where you spoke it
back when we didn't know how
there was time
there was time to try everything
every word
you spoke in me
hung in the air
clung to my limbs
like moss your words

we are damp as trees
we are swimming in a lake that swears it's a mirror
our arms thrown back
back
back
flap like wings
my face pokes from the lake like a mask
you inhabit my every breath

even today
i am growing old
but i know
i know what you like
i know what to do

GERALD NICOSIA

Ellen

Sunshine smile
Kind blue eyes
Gentle goodness deep inside—
A river of peace flows from your heart,
I'd like to rest there in the shade
For many and many and many a day.
I'd like to follow that river out
To whatever ocean your destiny holds.
I'd like to be a gentle rain
That keeps your river flowing

RODGER JACOBS

Pynchon at Craigville Beach

Thomas Pynchon had been engaged in a hard-fought wrestling match with a character in the new book he was writing; it was the central character, in fact, and the sonofabitch kept eluding Pynchon's descriptive skills.

Pynchon's wife offered a solution over breakfast one morning. She had made his favorite: pancakes shaped like rocket ships.

"I think the character sounds a lot like you," she said. "Just meditate on yourself in some abstract manner. Think about how you would describe yourself as a character."

After breakfast Pynchon felt a depression coming on. He decided to take a leisurely summer drive. That usually scared the darkening shadows away.

Before long Pynchon found himself on Route 6, headed into Cape Cod. He drove to Craigville Beach and parked the car in a public lot adjacent to the sand and surf. At Four Seas Ice Cream he pondered his wife's advice over a scoop of vanilla.

A stroll to the beach was in order after his tasty frozen treat. At the border where the asphalt met the wet sand, Pynchon removed his shoes and socks, placed them in one hand, and stepped into the cold, wet sand. He felt the sand squish between his toes.

He stood staring into the deep waters, trying to conjure up his qualities, both good and bad. He started with his physical qualities and didn't get very far. He was, he calculated, physically average for a man his age. Lifestyle? Nothing too lavish. Intellectual prowess? Well, that depends on what the critics and the academics are saying lately. But aside from his success as a novelist, everything else in his life came out to just about average. Normal. Healthy. Respectable. He was talented, yes, he knew that, but once he extracted that from the equation...

"Damn," he said with a sigh. "I'm nondescript."

DONNA HILBERT

Old Man at the Pool

What I knew about beauty,
the summer I turned ten,
I learned from books—
how Mammy squeezed Scarlett
into her corset for that famous
hand-span waist.
I was shaped like a milk carton.
I wore my mother's old merry widow
under my bathing suit
to push me up and cinch me in.

In the pool I played water babies,
pretending I was a creature
with no earthly life.
I sat on the bottom of the pool
until the need for air
propelled me to the surface
where I would turn over and over,
somersault into exhaustion.

I don't remember his face, just the gray
wires that grew down his belly
disappearing into his black trunks.
This old man, who held me
like a bowling ball,
his thumb in my crotch,
fingers splayed across
the bald arc of my pelvis,
this man who tossed me
into deep, deep water.

First published in *Deep Red* (Event Horizon, 1993)

BARBARA EKNOIAN

That Last Summer

We pushed off from the dock
in a canoe at dawn,
the sky blushing pink,
the lake water still as a pond,
no speedboats splashing by,
all the boat docks deserted
as vacationers were sleeping.

With every stroke of the paddle,
I noticed his strong muscles
and I knew I would miss
our tug of war trying to push
one another into the lake
in the evenings after supper.

The solitude was broken
when we laughed
as a muskrat swam by.
Then we glided
under the River Styx Bridge
to Byron's Cove,
where some huge estates
showed no signs of life.
We guessed the owners
had found more exotic places.

But I was so content to be there
on the lake
with my best summer buddy
for our last summer together
that I photographed
the landscape in my mind.
If it had not been so beautiful,
I would've forgotten it by now.

CAITLIN STERN

Heat Sink

As a child
I splashed and shouted in a pool with crowds
of other children
free during summer vacation
Every half-hour or so
I'd emerge
blue-skinned and trembling
and climb the playground's concrete vertical tube
yellow
and holed like Swiss-cheese
scrambling to the top
to plaster my damp skin against sun-warmed concrete
and bask in absorbed heat
before the sun
chased me
to cool chlorinated blue waters

Drift

Barefoot
wearing swimsuits and the occasional t-shirt
they relax into the cool embrace
of inflated rubber or vinyl
Some float alone
on a simple black circle
hands and feet dangling
Others yoked in pairs
or groups
carrying along coolers
cup holders
and conversations
Everyone drifts along a current
that carries on regardless
of its burden
They let the river take them
slow
steady
past rocky shore and trailing tree branches
by bobbing hopeful ducks
over the quicksilver flash of fish
and maybe catch
a nap

The Rope Swing

Sailing up, up into
Blue summer sky,
Hot rope rough against his hands,
He shouts with joy, and lets go.
For a crystal moment,
He hangs suspended,
Frozen in time
Like a fly in amber.
All awkward angles—
Shoulder blades and
Elbows, and
Knobby knees,
Painted against the sky,
Heart filled with fierce joy.

Dropping, down, down
Into clear green water
Cold on his skin,
He sinks to the silty bottom,
And sits suspended
In an alien world,
Watching the silvered flashes
Of tiny fish darting to and fro,
Startled by his sudden appearance.
I am a fish, too, he thinks,
And holds his breath
As long as he can.

Finally, he rockets up,
Through a stream of
Tickling bubbles,
Breaking the
Surface of the water
With a loud whoop of
Childish exuberance,
All thoughts of becoming a fish
Forgotten as he
Scrambles out,
            ➢

Shakes the water from his hair,
And, grinning, hitches up his
Baggy shorts.

He's ready
To do it all again.
Flying through the summer air,
Dropping into the cold water
To commune with fishes
Silvered in refracted light,
Then leaping to the surface,
A boy of ten once more,
Laughing through an endless summer
Made perfect by a cool green pond,
And an old rope swing.

CLINT MARGRAVE

I'll Tell You Why

I'll tell you why my father is a good man and to this day I will never think differently. My father is a good man because he could have lost it. He could have beaten the shit out of me and been forgiven by God and everybody else. He is a good man because now, even after all these years, I haven't forgotten.

It was summer. I had been swimming by myself all afternoon. I was waterlogged and a bit bored when I saw him step outside to have a smoke. Like any man, after a hard day's work, my father had a ritual when he got home. This ritual consisted of popping open a cold beer, turning on the sprinklers in the backyard, and relaxing in the late afternoon sun.

I'll tell you why my father is a good man, why my father belongs in the hall of fame for good men. Because honest-to-God, I didn't have bad intentions. The whole plan was innocent from the start. Up until the last moment, I honestly needed his help. And to this day, all I can tell you is that I don't know what made me do it.

There was a float I had dragged into the pool—a large one with drink holders and all that. I liked to surf on it. I liked to put the dog on it and swim around him like a shark. I liked to ride on it like it was my own ship. But that afternoon, I had other plans. I wanted to use it for a slide. I wanted to set it on the bond beam and slide down it into the pool. I needed help because I couldn't hold it and go down it at the same time. And this is why my father is a good man. Because he was gonna do it for me. Anything to please his only son. Anything to make his boy happy.

For months, I had dreamt about having my own slide. And now I found a temporary solution. It was simple. All he had to do was secure the back of the float while I slid down. My father had offered to help. Out of the kindness of his heart, my old man was gonna climb up there and hold the float. And let me tell you, he isn't the most coordinated man. He has never been one to play a sport. He is clumsy. He has trouble with his legs. But he was gonna help.

I pulled the float out of the water and climbed the steps to the bond beam. My father followed me, curious as to what I wanted from him. But I had it all mapped out. I would position the float over the edge of the bond beam like a slide, and as long as he kept the top steady, the plan would work. My father had agreed to do this. As tired as he was, as much as he wanted to rest, he had agreed to it. Dressed in his work clothes, cigarette still dangling in his mouth, trying to relax after a hard day's work, he had agreed. And to this day, all I can tell you is my intentions were good. To this day, all I can tell you is the plan was for him to hold the float and for me to slide down into the pool's deep end. Honest.

By this time, the float was positioned on the wet concrete at the top of the bond beam. Following my directions, he set his beer down and grabbed the top end of it.

Then something inside of me snapped.

I saw him positioned there, his feet spread apart on each end, his back bent with his hands gripping the center of the float, and I pushed him.

The next thing I knew, he was in the pool, his pockets filling with water, his pack of cigarettes ruined, all the money in his wallet soaking wet. I pushed my father into the pool in his dry-cleaned shirt, his slacks, his expensive shoes, his prescription glasses.

And I watched as he swam to the side, cursing under his breath, the hair he usually combed over his bald spot swinging down into his face. And I ran. I ran into the house, afraid of what he might do, realizing I had made one hell of a big mistake, feeling guilty, wishing only I could take it back. And I hid. I hid the best I could—first behind the closet door, then in the bathroom. As I heard footsteps coming up the stairs and my mother's voice screaming my name, I knew he was somewhere, recovering, waiting for his chance. I knew this was it. I had pushed my father too far. The father who was three times my size. The father who had only tried to help me.

And I cried. Partly from fear, partly from shame. Until my mom found me and sent me to my room without dinner, telling me the next few weeks were gonna be pretty lonely. And I cried even harder, either out of guilt or that the next few weeks were gonna be pretty lonely—I don't quite remember.

But I do remember the next time I saw him, he was dry. His hair was out of his face. He had a fresh pack of cigarettes. His pants were clean and his glasses once again rested comfortably across his face.

And to this day, all I can tell you is that my father is a good man. Because at that moment, he could have lost it. He could've beaten the shit out of me and God and everybody else would've forgiven him. He could've belted me pretty good. Instead, he just grinned, placed his hand on my shoulder, and promised to send me to military school if I ever did that again.

win harms

teenagers down the shore

memories of the ocean
sweet spring sweat trickles down my forehead
the sand stings my legs, as a crosswind
creeps up from behind
the salty sea is cold, numbing my bare feet
i hear my friends giggling ahead
and i laugh for no reason at all
you look at me and smile that secret smile
and for one moment we are alone in this
i can't remember the taste of you
but i know i'll understand you again
i get higher with the thoughts of days to come
we are sleepy with excitement
last night is so incredibly far away
we were older then, parading like sophisticates
we are young again, spinning in the sun
the past doesn't matter and
the skeletons don't feel like dancing
i am mapping out my life
and i want to see you there
with your eyes sparkling like the sea
we walk the boardwalk with the wind in our hair
creating everlasting impressions in time

JOAN JOBE SMITH

Endless Summers

Those endless summers when my son
and his buddies were too young
to drive a car, I packed as many
boy-men sardines that would fit
into my VW Bug and drove them
to the Surf Theater in Huntington Beach
to see surf movies, The Endless Summer,
Saltwater Wine and when the surf was Up,
they strapped as many surfboards as the VW
surf racks would hold and I drove them
to the Huntington Beach Pier where they
learned the poetry of the sea, sailed
aquamarine and spindrift soup
while I lay on the sand
studying for grad school exams
trying to make something of myself
and tried not to wish I were one of them
and then all the way home I listened to
their teen-aged a-b-c's of "awesome,"
"boss" and "cool," the salt and
sun turning their hair golden till
autumn and time to go back to school

and now my son and his buddies,
the age I was back then, their sun-streaked
hair grown-up dark while they try to make
something of themselves, come surfing now
to get back into shape and my son
brings his children now to show them
the way of the waves, those endless summers
and those sonnets of sun, sea and salt
going on and on as endless as
always.

First published in *Surfer* magazine (1997) and later published in *Pearl* (2000).

PART VI

MUSICAL INTERLUDE

My Judas

Let me rock you all night long
in the garden of thistles and thorns
where wild roses bloom.
Let me love you
back to the bend in the road
where you stared into a sky
sprawled with spiraling stars,
each light a simple wish
for a warm soul on a cold night.
Let me untangle the roots
of ancient conspiracy that
twist daylight into darkness,
making a palm itch
for thirty pieces of sliver.
Let me kiss your lips
before they betray the one you love.
Yet who am I to uncouple
your name with deceit?
We all dance with demons,
so be it, you are mine.

DAVID DONDERO

Summertime Suicide #1

That's how the song sings
When your heart begins this longing
One day it's a band of gold
Next day it's a chunk of coal
You like a harmony
I like a melody
That's you and me
We only disagree
That's how the song sings
It's how it sings
I like a bar with no TV
Tend to let a little conversation breathe
Keep your eyeballs glued to me
Undistracted by the TV screen
So you wanna talk
Wanna really talk
Well let's not talk
Not even say a thing
That's how the song sings
It's how it sings
You know I try to write a somber song
But I feel I've been away too long
Friends are grown and responsible
I'm a child yet not capable
That's how I come
That's how I go

That's how the song sings
When your heart begins this longing
One day it's a band of gold
The next day it's a chunk of coal

City Dance

I didn't know the slickery-slide of the city dance
The razzmatazz, the jazz
I didn't know the dance was going on
All the time
At sunrise, At morning coffee
At noontime Dim Sum
At night time poetry readings
Invisible tasting of bodies in a wine bottle
I hadn't learned to survive on scraps
A touch now and "when"
A leg too close
Thighs together on a coach
Body currents over a table
Everywhere the hunger
Men flirting with men
Women flirting with women
Men and women together
Those alone sing I-pads fingers to cooling the desire below
I was still longing for the old way
The moon, the swoon, spoons
The deep of yesterday
What a fool in this madness call day
And the insanity call night
Where one must go to the untouchables
The living and the dead
To breathe memories alive
Old Love, I have put you on a skewer
And roast you to just the right laughter
The perfect juiciness
Because you are too tasty to let go
Too enjoyable not to savor
As the juices runs down my face
I must learn to lower my head
So that love
Cannot be seen in my eyes
And dance the City dance
The City romance
And all that Razzmatazz
                    2/19/2013

LINDA KING

Danc'en Fool

You're on the floor
And you hear
The music throb'en
Beat'en and whirl'en
And you get in rhythm
Get a hold of it
Like a contest
With every instrument in the band
Beat with the drums
Strum with the guitar
Throb with the base
Sing with the fiddle
Everything in motion
Feet fly'en, arms in rhythm
Everything swing'en
With your partner
Stepp'en as one
Danc'en, follow'en
When you get
Your head swing'en
Your breasts flopp'en
Your eyes talk'en
Your hair churn'en
Your not a person
YOU'RE SONG
YOU'RE MUSIC
Your beat and sound and rhythm
All the tunes you've
Wanted to play
You're play'en
All the notes you've waned to sing
You're sing'en
But you're doing it with *body*
ALL TURNED LOOSE
EVERY PART ROLL'EN
AND MOV'EN AND PITCH'EN
AND CLIMAX'EN IN A FEVER OF MUSIC
HIS MUSIC, THEIR MUSIC, YOUR BODY MUSIC
GOD OH MIGHTY
THIS FOOL LOVES TO DANCE!!!

From *I Danced With a Man Last Night*

PART VII
JULY

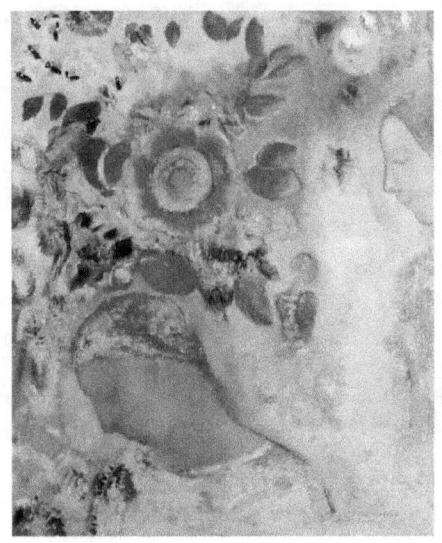

Tamara Madison

July Roses

Four stems
with four flowers each
crowd in a vase
like fatherless families
in a tenement house.
Thorny stems
must coexist
within this narrow tube
of water; it's difficult
but they resign to their fate.
By the time the youngest
opens lips to speak
Mother is in her blowsy prime
and the siblings
parade their promise
around the house
petals open to take in
the world, fluting outward
to share offerings
of scent and innocence.
As the babies part
sweet lips to sing
the mothers loose
upon the table
their own frazzled coifs
of pale petals,
displaying their tangles
of stamens as if to say
Yes, I am spent
but look what I have made!

DONNA HILBERT

Stephanie Who Is Twelve on the 4th of July

Stephanie who is twelve on the 4th of July
sits by herself on the curb:
palms pressed to cheeks, elbows on knees,

knees wide apart, (why, you can see her panties
from across the street). She's wearing her new
while dress, white pumps, white anklets.

The baby, babyish cousins wave sparklers
in the street while Uncle Mark lights
skyrockets, pinwheels.

Behind her, on the grass, her teen-age
cousins whisper "firecrackers,"
and "later." She wouldn't turn around—
not if you paid her.

Her aunts have been whispering all day
too, saying "her time," "breasts,"
and "trouble."
Stephanie presses her fingers to her eyes
until they throb and the stars are of her choosing.
Then she slips between the species
and trots off:
                    tossing her head,
tossing her head.

First published in *Mansions* (Event Horizons, 1990)

CAROLYN MILLER

A Warm Summer in San Francisco

Although I watched and waited for it every day,
somehow I missed it, the moment when everything reached
the peak of ripeness. It wasn't at the solstice; that was only
the time of the longest light. It was sometime after that, when
the plants had absorbed all that sun, had taken it into themselves
for food and swelled to the height of fullness. It was in July,
in a dizzy blaze of heat and fog, when on some nights
it was too hot to sleep, and the restaurants set half their tables
on the sidewalks; outside the city, down the coast,
the Milky Way floated overhead, and shooting stars
fell from the sky over the ocean. One day the garden
was almost overwhelmed with fruition:
My sweet peas struggled out of the raised bed onto the mulch
of laurel leaves and bark and pods, their brilliantly colored
sunbonnets of rose and stippled pink, magenta and deep purple
pouring out a perfume that was almost oriental. Black-eyed Susans
stared from the flower borders, the orange cherry tomatoes
were sweet as candy, the corn fattened in its swaths of silk,
hummingbirds spiraled by in pairs, the bees gave up
and decided to live in the lavender. At the market,
surrounded by black plums and rosy plums and sugar prunes
and white-fleshed peaches and nectarines, perfumey melons
and mangos, purple figs in green plastic baskets,
clusters of tiny Champagne grapes and piles of red-black cherries
and apricots freckled and streaked with rose, I felt tears
come into my eyes, absurdly, because I knew
 that summer had peaked and was already passing
away. I felt very close then to understanding
the mystery; it seemed to me that I almost knew
what it meant to be alive, as if my life had swelled
to some high moment of response, as if I could
reach out and touch the season, as if I were inside
its body, surrounded by sweet pulp and juice,
shimmering veins and ripened skin.

From *Light, Moving*. ©Sixteen Rivers Press, 2009. Reprinted with permission.

Summertime Suicide #2

Ice cream and lemonade
Watermelon at the big parade
Explosions in the sky
Favorite day is on the 4th of July

'Cause the Schiefelbeins
had a pontoon boat
with a barbeque grill
they kept the barbeque afloat
all the while pulling Charlie around
on his inflatable donut

Manjares and the party starts
Badminton and
we ride the go-carts
Hannahlee's on the trampoline
with her super-soaker

While the old men
are playing horseshoes
All the young boys
wearin' no shoes
Slidin' crazy down a slip-n-slide
It's a summertime suicide

Tiki torches and citronella candles
Fireflies and birdlike mosquitoes
Feel a chill from an oscillating fan
Feel your sunburn become a suntan
Good times we've had
but there's too many
good times to come

GERALD LOCKLIN

Edward Hopper: Summertime (Revisited)

I could study this canvas everyday
And write a different poem from it.

Today's is about the daring exposure
Of her nipples and thighs
And even the red thatch between the latter
Through the airy thinness of her sundress.

Hopper's blue is often almost white.
Her posture and her parted lips
Declare our unbowed determination
Undiminished by the years, as late as 1943,
When an entire nation fought
A war upon two fronts,
And prevailed on both.
This red-lipped woman going forth
To meet all comers in her straw hat,
Flowing locks, strong biceps, trim waist,
And foot-forward was a reincarnation
Of Liberty, the Second Coming of
The Lady in the Harbor with the Torch of Freedom,
She also a standard-bearer of our Greatest Generation.

Erika Spray Paints Till Dawn

Late July and the night
moves restless. Under the
bright moon, 6 coyotes
and a Union Pacific freight
carry on in milky light.
I lie in bed, one hand at my heart,
the other on private equipment.
It's a good sign. It means
I might live.

You say, "It's a good night to
spray paint some furniture."

I think when both hands are at the heart
they may have been placed there
by a third party.
I've never trusted that.

It's better when elements
line up and circumstances
lend themselves. We know
there is a right time,
a perfect time,
and tonight, in this pale
rustling light, spray paint
in turquoise
and never forget.

Let no distance obscure
this turquoise.
In my mind
there is you
pressing a little red button
and making turquoise
in the night. And
in a noisy July dawn
a storage cabinet
glows turquoise
glows quiet.

TERE SIEVERS

July Rain

The sudden storm
flashes and rumbles
the ozone air a tonic
for the humid afternoon.

I stand waiting
at the screen door
as the hard rain digs
puddles in the dirt.

I remember July,
the hot Jersey summers
mud under my feet
thick, warm and soft.

Now, I open the door
smell the air
drop my shoes
and step into the rain.

A Queer Bashing

> *"All You Need Is Love"*
>
> THE BEATLES

I

You want to know how it was?
I parted my hair for a girl that morning,
4th of July.
She wore a black two-piece, boobs like
Marilyn. I wore surfer trunks, all this
to please the family.

II

Teenaged feet shattered my glasses,
blood on the parking pavement, alone,
my eye a battered vessel,
windowshield wiper bent,
a broken finger where queers hang out,
a penis burned by a coiled lighter.

The radio circulated Beatles, pollen
powdered my stung eyes, an ambulance
arrived too late at the hospital door,
a socket too obvious to mention,
a blister too swollen to bandage,
a song too pungent to believe.

From *Moonman: New and Selected Poems* (World Parade Books, 2012)

SYED AFZAL HAIDER

Invisible Presence

The picture—a memory of light
Treasured by the shadow.

RABINDRANATH TAGORE

Looking at the photograph stuck on the kitchen refrigerator with a round blue magnet of Diane, Damien, and Destiny from two years ago that I took on Damien's third birthday, June 21, Damien asks, "Daddy! Why was my mommy laughing?"

Smiling back at dear Diane in the portrait of our family, I say, "Maybe she was happy." It was a joyous occasion.

After years of trying for a second child, Diane and I were content with being one-child parents. We were blessed with Damien, our unexpected bundle of joy. Diane was thirty-six, our daughter Destiny was eleven, and I was forty.

I refill my cup of coffee. We sit down on kitchen table, Damien with bowl of Cheerios without milk and me with a cup of coffee, black, and Sunday *Daily News*.

"Didn't she know she was going to die?" he continues.

"I don't think so."

"How did she die?"

"Her boat sank."

"Did she fall in the water?" Concern in his voice.

"I'd think so."

"That must have been scary," he says in a low voice.

"Must be," I say, looking down at Sunday *Daily News*.

℘

Two years ago on Fourth of July, Diane went sailing from Sunset Beach on my friend and fellow psychiatrist, Marty Silverman's catamaran, *Splendor*, with seven other women. Destiny was away on a camping trip in Sierra Blanca, New Mexico. I took Damien to his first baseball game, Giant vs. Cubs.

Sitting in bleacher seats, Damien and I eat peanuts and hot dogs, I let Damien drink cola, which Diane would not permit, but I thought it was an especial occasion, Father and Son bonding. I drank Anchor Steam. The game was not that exciting. They hit with vim; we hit with whimper.

At the end of the seventh, a full moon glows brightly over the center field. The Giants are losing eight to three. We leave our seats to buy Damien a souvenir. He wants a catcher's mitt. We walk from one stall to another, covering all the bases, but the end result remains the same. They don't have one right-hand glove for a lefty in his size.

When we return to our seats, the dark clouds have enveloped the full moon; the wind has shifted, blowing with high velocity from home plate towards bleachers. Winning with force and fluke, we win ugly, nine to eight, in the bottom of the ninth, and the Giants score six runs, hitting two solo home runs and one grand slam.

The crowd is jubilant singing, "Hey! Hey! Goodbye." I turn and smile at Damien and notice that he's crying. Unhappy, he didn't get his mitt. His sobs get louder. There is so much excitement that no one can hear him. "Hey! Hey! Goodbye!" Warm, blustery airstream roars with lightning and thunder. The ballpark glows like a spaceship under the dark clouds. We leave exhausted, soaking in sweat and covered in dust. Damien keeps weeping, making gasping sounds, on the way to our car.

"Can I do anything to make you feel better?" I ask.

"No, nothing," he snivels. "I like being sad and poor."

"Why?"

"There are no 'whys'," he says, serious.

"How come?" I pursue.

"I don't know." He shakes his head. "I just do."

"But we are not poor."

"I feel sad," he says.

"That can't be helped," I say, buckling his seatbelt. "Feelings change. No state of mind is permanent."

A heavy rain begins to fall, and it hails and rains all the way, 101 to 17, to our exit, Water Street.

When we arrive home, Springsteen is singing, "(*There is)* Darkness On The Edge Of Town." A full moon is shining brightly over our dark house. We sit in the car until the song ends. I get out, walk around, and open the car door for Damien.

We walk in; it is dark everywhere.

଼

Diane and her party never returned from their sailing. Their boat capsized. According to the news reports, in hail and rain and high winds, a speedboat went out of control and hit *Splendor* like a torpedo on the mark, killing everyone on board. Instant death. No survivors. They never found the body of Patricia Hirsch, Marty's woman, his mate.

଼

"Daddy, you're not listening to me!" screams Damien.

"I am," I say, looking up from Sunday *Daily News*. I sense his sadness, or my sadness reflected in him. Having spent one lifetime learning to leave, and another moving from place to place, I just want to get home.

"You're not," says Damien firmly, tears in his eyes.

"Maybe. Maybe." I repeat, looking at Damien, I say, "Come here, Noodles, I want to hug you."

I sit him on my lap. He looks at me. "How old was I when I stopped drinking milk from my mommy?"

"Your mommy breastfed you for six months, then when she went back to work she breastfed you once in the morning and once at night until you were one year old," I say.

"How did my mother talk?"

How does one describe a person's talk, their voice? Does a flower sigh when it blossoms? I don't answer. He asks an easier question.

"What did my Mommy do?"

"She was a movie critic," I answer.

"Did she like movies?"

"Yes," I say, with lots of enthusiasm. "She loved movies."

"I like movies," he says.

Life is a movie. I thought. It plays on.

ʒα

I am weeding in Diane's garden. Green has turned to dust. It is time to close the season of loss and regrets. Damien and Destiny walk out of our house. Damien wants to know if I want to bike down to the beach with them.

"Not now," I say. "Maybe later I'll walk over and meet you."

"Dad! Come along now," says Destiny "We won't be gone long."

"Work before pleasure," I say, smiling.

"All work, no pleasure," says Destiny as she and Damien bike away

Too much to do, I don't get anywhere, not enough time. I can't get focused. I don't stay on the task. I walk away from things. I leave things undone. My right shoulder is hurting. Something is always out of sync.

Leaving a pile of leaves in the driveway, I walk to Sun Splashed Beach.

Hot and sunny, it's windy at the beach. High tides are rolling in. People soaking up sunshine. I walk with a sense of purpose looking for Damien and Destiny. Joey, kindergarten mate of Damien's dressed in a black Batman T-shirt and black shorts, comes running towards me. I see his parents, Ira and Joan Levine, lying on a large yellow beach towel, trying to get a tan.

"Is your mother dead?" Joey asks, without waiting a moment.

What a crazy world we live, I think. "Yes," I say, looking away, hoping to spot Damien and Destiny.

"How did she die?" he asks.

"She was old and sick," I say. Do I tell him about my mother's battle with breast cancer?

"Did someone shoot her?" asks Joey.

This boy wants details. "No." I am brief.

"Did her sailboat drown?" he asks.

Shaking my head, looking at the rising waves. I say, "You have been talking about Damien's mother."

"Yeah," says Joey innocently. "You're the dad and she was the mommy."

"You're absolutely right," I say, matter of fact. "Damien and I have both lost our mommies."

"I know," says Joey sounding sad.

"Have a good day," I say, walking away from Joey. There was no point in asking him if he has seen Damien.

I walk back from the beach, wondering if I had answered all of Joey's questions. Did I answer them correctly? Did he have more questions?

Destiny's and Damien's bikes are sitting at the end of the driveway when I arrive home. The pile of leaves that I left behind has been blown by the wind, shrunken low, like a bed for someone to lie down and die.

121

CR

Tomorrow is Fourth of July, the third anniversary of Diane's death. Why make a big deal of it? The loss is already there. It's history, all done and gone, a time for quiet remembrance. Restless and uneasy, with little to do, I work lazily in Diane's garden. I loosen the dirt. Weed the unwanted green. Her garden is gone mad, wild and out of control. The wilderness is unlimited. Flowers do blossom in the ruins. I am with Diane, but she is not with me. Destiny knows that tomorrow is the anniversary of her mother's death but we don't talk about it, she acts grown up, and I let her be. Damien does not. One can celebrate death every day and there is Day of Dead and the day we die. My hands are cold, covered with dirt; my blue jeans are dirty, my knees and back are hurting. I can't lift my right arm. I feel a chill in the air. I cut blue, white, and yellow gladioli and put them on the kitchen table in a blue ceramic vase that Diane bought at *New Era: All Things Old,* her favorite rummage shop. I look out of the kitchen window it begins to rain. Diane is never coming home.

CR

The Fourth of July turns cool and cloudy, with a chance of rain. In the afternoon, Destiny takes Damien to Sophia's so they can play. Damien is getting to be a big boy now; he's beginning to have his own friends.

It stops raining early in the evening. There is one rainbow than another, Destiny and Damien insist on going to Marty's new boat, docked at Municipal Harbor. Marty lost Patricia Hirsch, his live-in partner in the same boating accident that killed Diane. Marty wants to move on. I say more power to him. Marty has decided to live again. I second that notion. "It's Patricia who died, not I," he says. What could be more factual and truthful? It has been three long years, and Patricia is not coming back, he says, and he is right about that as well. Mary Wayne, Marty's newly found woman friend, a professional nurse, is an elegant English woman. She speaks perfect French also. She giggles each time she says *oui* to whatever Marty whispers in her ear.

On cool evening, on board Marty's new boat, *New Beginnings,* Mary is entertaining. She wears a black silk dress and cultured pearl necklace, serving Piña Coladas and sushi.

"I find no need to believe in anything," says Marty. "It's the meaninglessness of life that makes me sad."

I take my first big bite of *ika* and turn to Marty, my eyes full of tears from too much *wasabi*, and we both start laughing.

Surrounded by gray clouds above, the fog around, and the silver lining in the distant horizon, the fireworks start. The colors are faint and muted, misty, obscure, and dim in the dense fog. It creates a strange psychedelic visual effect. It doesn't seem real, like the dreams of a drunken sailor.

The twelfth symphony, Overture 18, is playing. The fireworks are coming to a finale. I see a blissful Marty with his hand around Mary's waist. I watch a joyous Damien holding Destiny's hand. It's all good. It is as is. I see the reflections of the fireworks in the sea, colorful like Diane's garden full of flowers on a cloudy morning before the sunrise.

MARCIA MEARA

The Last Rose

Late July, and
The day drowses,
Air heavy and still.
Bees moving slowly from
Flower to flower,
In a dance weighed down by heat.
Sleepy hours spent dreaming, longing
For other places, other chances.
Anything better
Than one more day
Spent under this weight,
With movements made slow,
Like easy prey.

He walked out of the dust
And into the garden,
The answer to a prayer.
Wickedly handsome, he came to her with
A smile full of promises she chose to believe.
Take me away, she begged.
Yes, he whispered, of course.
Whatever you want, my beautiful girl.
He gave her dreams of cool, green hills
And kisses that tasted of summer peaches.
Sweet lies on a sweeter tongue,
Promises whispered with hot breath,
Against already burning skin,
And everywhere, the smell of roses
Thick on the summer air.

But winter came,
Bringing brittle wind
Seeping under the sill,
As cold as hungry lies
Told when the sun was warm.
Her heart is a frozen stone
In the center of her breast,
➢

The chance of rescue,
Gone. Forgotten.
A faded rose in a dry vase
Drops one last petal to the floor,
As gray as her life
In this barren room.
Empty promises fled
With the summer sun,
And left nothing behind
But dead dreams and dying hope,
Gasping and huddled
Against the bitter
Cold.

PART VIII
LIGHT & DARK

JASON PARKER

Soaking Up the Sun

Excerpt from the Novel *Soul Synthesis*

Little did the swarm know: this world we are a piece of had only been this way roughly fifteen percent of its little galactic existence. What we had grown so comfortable with and accustomed to as normal absolutely was not. It was no wonder everything was changing. And rapidly at that. We were coming out of the hibernation of another ice age. Just as natural and inevitable as anything else. We clung to the past like some kind of rogue lover. She didn't call. She didn't even care. She simply moved on to the next one. The future was happening whether we liked it or not and there was nothing we could do about it but pretend to enjoy the ride. Yet that certain something that made us whole was dwindling and eventually missing. Something you could maybe call stability. There was only one thing left and we were approaching it like a waterfall in the rapids. Some people put their hands up and smiled. Others let go or wrapped their arms around those closest to them not knowing what else to do.

I remember the day I was lying naked in my backyard with her soaking up the sun. She asked me if I ever wanted to have kids some day. After rolling the question around like a couple of dice for a second I replied.

"I think it's basically the reason why we are here."

We just lay there. Flipping over from time to time. Drinking water with our sunglasses on.

Time passed like sandpaper on my soul. There was a part of me that felt the urge to do this more than anything. But there was another part of me that rang an alarm at the top of the tower calling down to me shouting:

"How could you bring another one of you into this world? We don't stand a chance!" I drank salty tears in the afternoon not knowing what to think as the poles of possibility oscillated back and forth.

I find myself among them. The masses. If they can do it, so can I. Some of the world's leading geneticists propose that we as a whole are only decreasing in our intelligence despite all of our knick-knacks and gadgets. If that's the case, then there might as well be at least some of us here to continue thinking and continue inspiring those around us. Even if it may seem like there is no place for us here. We've made it this far with our history and our womb's pursuit. Even if the plug has been pulled and the tub of water is only draining. Or should I say melting? There should still be some of us here trying no matter what happens. I see no other reason to exist other than to make this happen. As utterly ridiculous and tragic as it may seem, this is what we are.

You can break things down however far you want to. Everything you ever think and are is your creation. It is up to you. Sure things will happen along the way. But those are speed bumps that act as our only challenge left. You simply cannot hand over a paradise and expect it to always be that way. These moments were something to be cherished, not used. Everything is temporary. We can give in and curl up into a little ball and try to hide. We can do the best we can and have fun with it. We aren't going to be here much longer. How much of your life have you already lived? You might be over half way there. You might be dead tonight when you close your eyes to dream. Did you follow your heart? Did you do what you feel is right? Did you hold yourself back?

Fear was like a fire that escaped the stained glass lantern of the heart's golden cathedral. It made it seem as if it was lighting the way. But it was burning everything we had left. We obeyed its sanction of safety and I will no more. There is no reason to. You couldn't convince me with any sort of numbers or language. I see it feeding off of us like a machine of leeches in the sky of the quantum mind. For those who think we serve no purpose and simply wound up here randomly, I commend you. You are the kinetic energy being harvested for next round. No matter the space or time we think is between us, I love you.

KAREN MARGOLIS

Berlin Year 2 A.W.*
        * A. W. = After the Wall

1.

There's a poem in the fridge lying just below the icebox
I put it there to cool off
three weeks past now
the one-eyed mackerel is reading it sideways
and the fifth line is suffering from frostbite

2.

What hope for this land
with the mailboxes yellow
the moon masculine
and everyone straining, straining
so hard to grow up

3.

The air full of the cries of reborn egos
pollution index 22, rising: another reason
not to get up
                    you tell me per FAX
the future will be read
in the weather report; walking
the Kantstrasse the pavements turn to bread
soggy in the post spring shower
low and hi fi collide: occluded depression
before the shop sign Früchte aus aller Welt
they devalued the banana made whips
of its skin, rechanneled the Spree, then
eliminated unemployment at a stroke
with the ultimate olympic project
of the final ideological conquest:
operation solar reversal
target date 31 Dec. 1999
the sun shall sink in the east.

4.

Looking for the corner
waiting for the word to click
once the word was wall or border
you could blow it up in your head

5.
Walking fast
so as not to see
talking fast
so as not to hear
eating fast
so as not to taste
fucking fast
so as not to feel
greeting fast
so as not to touch
shitting fast
so as not to smell
working fast
to beat the race
spending fast
to compensate
fast fast faster fastest
after death comes time

6.
After the wall went down
there was nothing (left) to do
                              but wait
for the poles to melt

state of the city (running report)

political assassinations
economic motivations
motorbiked policemen in green leather
the right righteous
the left embarrassed
the president religiously
inclined to white-haired dignity
state funeral   state theatre
sunshine inappropriately
illuminating top security
pistols at half cock
flags at ditto mast
ceremony clothes the fear
they missed the chance
to wrap the Reichstag
so burying the Treuhand boss
they throw clods of regret
on the coffin; yet another
opfertäter bites the dust
a handful of soft hands are washed
with Ph neutral liquid soap
and the work goes on
the rapid unwinding
of the bandages of a million mummies
that Egypt won't take back
for love or money
—though they're now free
to take a boat trip down the Nile
view the Elgin marbles
and get lost in the Knossos labyrinth
but— despite heavy advance booking—
there will be no tours, guided
or otherwise through the Stasi archives
except for those
who know it all already
apart from details, names
and suchlike. But why drag the past
into the presence of those
who actually lived it
as theirs not to reason why.
political machinations
sombre incantations

a polar high blesses Berlin
pavement café tables mushroom
the Poles who braved the frontier stoning
wander dazed, the West is tamed
eldorados sidewalks swell
the Indian roseseller peels away
the browning petals
to press into the hand
of the Rumanian gypsy
who hands her note—in Deutsch—
to the Javanese businessman
while the children plead big-eyed
as they've been taught to do
by family and life

political accusations
property speculation
spaghetti al pesto consumed al dente
outside the pizzerias under the sunshades
the right established
the left: left aside
the president courageously ignoring
the stink of the Brandenburg dung
retiring again for handwashing
last rites, ritual repetition
—'rituals are essential
especially for children'—
what! will these little hands
never be clean?
out damned spot   sheathe the dagger
shelve the Damoclean sword
in the library of Schloß Glienicke
first nights, past repressions
three opera houses ample compensation
for roof cracks in the Philharmonic Hall
and last but not late a statement
to the press: noses to the grindstone
hands to the plough
faithful hands, right hands
pulling together, the knots
unravel so easily now
there are no more conspiracy
theories   only
thoughts of French origin
on the velocity of images
...tempus fugit...pensée retrouvée ...
and the necessity of war

for mass communication
when the weather, being predictable
loses its talking-point value.
at 25 Marks a kilo the green silk scarf
weighing in at less than a feather
cost next to nothing.
lilacs on the other hand
get dearer all the time—
April again: that PS TS
wand'ring in the wasteland
polyphonic longing for a ragtime band
Eliot the poet
for the thinking man.

political calculations
polemical associations
the polar high progressing nicely
put on the last summer sunglasses
wind the green scarf round the throat
(there is no right or wrong)
prepare for the Friday supermarket
one can never be too careful

as the president said
and it was only Tuesday then
we Germans
still have thin skins
you too? and you? and you?
—maybe but don't mean me
when they say wir Deutschen bei uns etc.
I switch off /being extraterritorial
at any rate he couldn't have meant either
the man in the grey suit
Ku'damm ecke Knesebeck
standing at the Imbiss
eating a Wiener sausage
complete with intestinal coating
and mustard enough
to kill all known germs.

ja, the skin is thin
myself, I've been without
since Elke said, we're all skinless
in that vague myopic way of hers
that always homes in
on matters of the heart
—and that was a year ago now—

footnote:
it was one of those days
which on waking I wanted
to consign
to the dustbin of history

it was saved by the bell
Mercury on a bicycle, meaty thighs
missive from the Akademie (West)
who pays the piper
calls the poetess to order

ordered translations
economic motivations
ponderous implications of artistic import
the thoughts that count
(69 lines á 2.20 per line
                = 151.80
+ Value Added Tax)
subject: the special location
film fantasy the guiding theme
the city offers bunkers
no mans wastelands
Gründerzeit villas (and) here
and there a slum or two
more than enough for a movie set
with a growing pool of unemployed
extras   tougho youngsters
specialist condom shops
& streetgirls in spacesuits
plus the aftermath
of a 40-year experiment
in social architecture
engineering & steering
all of which translated
bodes well for business
(relatively speaking) and not badly
for state subsidised bodies
sociologists, semiologists, psychologists
and waitresses

but brings of course a calculated risk
of political assassinations

ja, the skin is thin
when a bomb splinter pierces
a bullet passes quite easily through
the Bulgarians however went one better
they did it with an umbrella

the rosy rollercoastin' cost of
livin' lovin' & givin'

a rose on the schönhauser allee
costs as much now for the worker bees
oozing out of the s-bahn
as a line of translation typed out korrektly:
two and a half D-marks precisely
(and-don't-subtract-the-value-added-tax)

still and all today that's cheaper
than the blackmarket fag packets
laid out in blankets on the pavement
at the feet of the vietnamese poor
veteran cousins, faces wary
the last remaining loose
change of socialist relations

in the stinky subway passage
beneath the scrawl message
hitler lives, the lonesome saxophone
bleats out a barely audible survival blues

The Dawn of Reality

One by one,
at the fag end
of a grey English summer,
winter wagging a grizzled toe
through the same pair
of worn-out shoes,
life peeled away
my most cherished illusions.

Cities and towns,
their remembered charms
sadly tarnished
in the cold glare
of a half-hidden sun,
stood naked and freezing
in their concrete bones,
fool's gold
alchemized into basest iron,
rusting
under the dying strands
of a melting rainbow.

Worse still,
like good wine turned sour
in the stale air of liquid time,
friends and lovers became themselves.

The Deep Sleep, or an Accidental Moment Revealed

It had been hours since Thanksgiving dinner and everyone was still full of good food, drink and family chatter. With the table finally cleared, the older kids disappeared in search of their friends while the younger two scurried downstairs for some long-awaited computer time. My husband was happily hibernating in his home office, thankful to be left alone for a few hours of solitude.

With the soft whir of the dishwasher playing its mechanical tune in the background, I opened the refrigerator and tossed in the final containers of leftovers, secretly hoping to never see them again.

Satisfied with how the day had passed, I grabbed my glass of wine and headed into the living room. My mother was curled up in the corner of the sofa; tightly wound in several blankets with only her head poking out over the top folds. She had deposited herself there nearly an hour before, patiently waiting to watch an old episode of *Boston Legal* that she had requested I record the night before.

Request is really a funny way to put it because she had been insistent that I not forget to record it. In fact, she talked about it ad nauseam—even after I assured her that I had checked the DVR and it had successfully programmed. At dinner, the kids painstakingly tried to explain digital recordings, but to no avail. Since we couldn't produce a VHS tape to give her tangible evidence, she assumed it just didn't really exist. No matter, I was about to allay her fears.

"Okay, ready?" I said as I grabbed the remote and plunked down beside her.

"I've been ready for over an hour," she said with a smile that belied her ribbing. "I'm not getting any younger, you know."

"No, but I am," I joked. "Haven't I told you about my Dorian Gray picture-in-the-attic thing?"

"Shhhhhh," she said as the first scenes of the show flickered to life.

I settled back and pondered this phenomenon. It might have taken me awhile but as I aged, I finally gave up critiquing my mother's rigid schedule, having fallen victim to my own rising insecurities. Portrait in the attic aside, I no longer pretended I could remember daily minutiae: if I had taken my vitamins that morning or if I had left the teapot boiling. (I gave up and bought an electric kettle that automatically shut itself off to avoid exactly this dilemma). I didn't snap every time she said, "Just wait until you're my age," and didn't always reply with the standard retort, "You're still as sharp as ever, Mom." No matter how old we get, everyone still hates insincerity, no matter how well intended.

As I watched my own crow's feet deepen, my empathy for her vulnerabilities also increased in equal amounts. A widow for over twenty years, she was still sharp and pretty and often courted by the elderly men who lived in her complex.

"I'm seventy-five, and I just don't need the hassle," she'd say emphatically. "Even though I hate being alone, I don't want to date." And with that the conversation was over.

So stay single she did. She lived alone, traveled with groups of women, took care of friends, and tirelessly volunteered.

I suppose this snowed me. Because of her energetic life I failed to see her as old. After all, she's your mom. She might be older, but never *really* old.

So I kicked off my shoes and watched while William Shatner and James Spader went splashing into the ocean, arm-in-arm. It was a special *Boston Legal* episode, their "Summer Snaz" show where Shatner walks around the office in scuba gear and a flamboyant wetsuit, while Spader plays an enviable sidekick complete with rubber ducky. I chuckled and glanced over to see her reaction. But what I saw was that she was asleep. Not just snoozing, but fast asleep. So I pushed "pause" on the remote, and I paused to deliberate. Recalling that she really wanted to see this program, I decided to wake her up. At first she was startled but then insisted that she really wasn't asleep, only resting her eyes. I didn't argue, but merely continued the program.

We watched together until the first commercial break. But by the time the ads had finished, she was snoring again. So once more I hit "pause." I waited ten minutes and decided to try one more time. I softly nudged her arm, waking her slightly.

"Mom, do you want to go to bed or would you like to see your show?" She blinked herself awake.

"Oh, of course I want to see the show," she said trying to shake off her sleep. "I was just waiting for you."

I pressed play. And within minutes, I was watching and she was sleeping. Without ceremony, I shut off the TV and let the blissful silence take over the room.

But a peculiar thing happened. Unlike the many other times she would fall asleep in front of the TV, I didn't read a book or a magazine, or get up to do a chore. This time I just sat and watched her sleep. Maybe this was odd but it was something I felt compelled to do.

And even more curious, I found myself traveling to another universe in another era. It was almost as if I were trying to make a mental scrapbook of the past. In my mind's eye, could I remember when her hair was dark, not white, or when her face was smooth, not creased? I must admit, I was having a bit of trouble with that, but what I vividly remembered were sharp snapshots of long ago: her petite frame balancing a full basket of washed clothes as she glided towards the clothesline on a warm summer's day, her patiently standing in the bathroom crisscrossing bobby pins to make spit curls around her face or the pungent smell of Noxema wafting through the house every evening. I can still see her watching an egg timer while standing over a whistling pressure cooker or lying on the floor in front of a tiny black-and-white TV bumping along to Jack LaLanne. I remember her sitting on a sofa cushion to peer over the steering wheel of a monstrously large station wagon in a candy-striped outfit on her way to the hospital.

Contemplating this, I sipped my wine and listened to the sounds of my city apartment coming to a rest at the end of a day. And then, a thought I never allowed myself to think surfaced: how many more Thanksgivings might I have like this?

About an hour later, I woke her for the third time and quietly told her it was time to go to bed. This time she didn't protest and allowed me to lead her away.

As you could guess, the next day she chided me unmercifully for letting her sleep, but I just let it go. That afternoon, she watched her long-awaited episode while I went to work. She was miffed that it happened this way.

The following Tuesday, I put my mom on a plane and she flew back home. She phoned when she arrived to tell me the frozen soup I had sent with her survived the trip.

A week later, while wrapping Christmas gifts, my mother passed away from a brain aneurysm. Just like that, just that quickly. The surgeon comforted me by insisting that she died quickly and without pain.

Still, I wondered; did I know without knowing?

Today, I sat in the corner of the sofa where my mom last dozed and thought about watching her sleep. For now this memory has usurped all the others. I realized it's not about what I will remember, but rather, what I know I won't forget: the silence, the peacefulness of sitting next to a woman I had known for fifty-three years…of being close without touching, of feeling secure and safe and loved.

Ah, the dominoes of life slowly tipping one against the other. And I hope that one day when I'm curled up on my daughter's sofa they might know just how important an accidental moment can become.

And believe it or not, I'm starting to question if I really want my picture to stay in the attic after all.

MORIAH LACHAPELL

Needles

During the summer of 1988
my Mother, at 36 lay dying
in the blue room
at the Ranch
of a brain tumor
after the second surgery.

Her craniotomy carved
a hellish Mohawk.
In her morphine state,
she said *I am just driving in to New York.*

Grandma said God had the mercy
to taking her traveling.
Starlings sang in the pine trees
on a July day in the Central Valley.
Where else would she want to be?
As her four children played
outside, they have not brushed
their teeth for weeks.

MORIAH LaCHAPELL

Dear Shannon

I received your very nice and most welcome letter
sent to me by you July 18th.
This letter will not arrive on your birthday.
I do however convey to you all my love
and trust you had a very lovely birthday.

You are surely fast becoming a young lady
of twelve years, past the age now
when I can give you the bum's rush.

It will not be long until I will
have to tip my hat to you
and even perhaps send you
pretty clothes.

Steven and Kevin will both go
to Marymount School.
I would like very much
for you to go away
to a real nice girls school.
I am very anxious that you
and all your brothers and sister
attend very good schools
that will prepare you all
for a very fine education.

It is nice of you to say you miss me
and I miss you sweetheart very much.

I am happy you are enjoying your vacation.
You say you have a tan so that means
you have had plenty of sun.
I too hope you enjoy San Francisco.

It was a very great loss for me to lose Dorothy
and to be away from all things
that every day reminded me of her.

I am sure it was good for me.

This letter is not a birthday present
as you requested it to be.
It will not be too long until I will see you
and then we will select a very lovely birthday present.

Be a real nice girl,
I know you attend church regularly
and pray for your Daddy in heaven.
I will close with all my love to you.
It is not necessary to save this letter.

NOTE: This poem is based on a letter to my mother from her Uncle Dave Beck, president of the Teamsters Union before Jimmy Hoffa. Uncle Dave wrote the letter during 1963 while in prison at McNeil Island Penitentiary for pocketing $1,900 from the sale of a union-owned Cadillac. In 1975, President Gerald Ford pardoned him. His wife Dorothy died while he was serving his sentence.

Glass

Things were kept under glass in my grandmother's house. The statue of the Infant Jesus of Prague and the clock on the mantelpiece were protected from grandchildren's sticky fingers under glass domes. A seahorse that belonged to my uncle who had died in the war rested in a glass box behind the glass doors of the hallway desk, right next to the glass globe that featured tiny houses and a star in the sky and snow when you turned it upside down. Watercolors of birch trees that my artistic aunts had painted in their youth were flattened behind panes of glass and hung everywhere.

All these and more were kept behind glass in our small space on this street in this town in this state in this country on this continent on this planet in this solar system in this galaxy, behind glass windows that were loose in their frames and shook and rattled at the slightest breeze. Sometimes all the glass in this house jangled and groaned at once, from high-pitched to low, like water-filled glasses struck with a knife.

As a visitor, as a stayer in my grandmother's St. Louis apartment during the summer, there were chores, there were rules, there were lessons. There was time to fill. There were many evenings of watching buses from the front porch, the glass rattling behind me as I sat outside, tinkling from a rare breeze or from the four-flat settling in its foundation.

We worked, so the time to fill would be less. We ironed everything. The angles of a white handkerchief against the gray ironing board, the curves of tablecloths, the legs of our underwear. We dedicated ourselves here, studied these angles and curves and contrasts of color as the glass rattled—time passing—our marking the movement of it in sheets and pillowcases.

The heat kept us inside, pushed us back as we wandered out to get the mail or retrieve the day's milk or throw crusts to the birds. Back inside, into that space, those rooms allotted for us to spend our time and scrub the back of Revere Ware pots with kitchen cleanser.

Between scrubbing and sweeping, we looked for things to do. We did jigsaw puzzles of red barns and tulips in Holland and the Eiffel Tower in Paris. We played Honeymoon Solitaire. We watched *The Price is Right* on television and vacuumed and dusted when there was no dust.

We watched nature programs and Mr. Wizard, who taught us how to make a terrarium. We used an old chipped plate with Mexican sombreros on it for the bottom and bought a glass dome at the dime store, along with small plants in white square plastic pots. We went to the pet supplies section and purchased plaster houses intended for fish tanks. Then we went home and searched through the Christmas boxes in the basement and found tiny people and houses that went with my dead uncle's Lionel train set.

We followed Mr. Wizard's instructions about soil and water and arranged it all just so on our sombrero plate. Then with great ceremony we placed the glass dome on top of the small world and enclosed it. Now we had something to look at during the late afternoons, a small world watering itself. A new piece of glass to clink as we walked past.

Also in that house lived my uncle who had survived the war. He went from the Army to the Postal Service—I think he liked the uniforms. As he ascended the stairs to our second floor flat each late afternoon, he's say, "I'm home," and I'd peek from behind the banister and see his green tongue as he opened his mouth to announce his arrival.

Each day, I asked why his tongue was green and each time he replied that he had been eating grass, at which I would park myself in a corner of the hallway and wait to be called to supper. I have a Mad Uncle, I thought. A Mad Uncle who gobbles grass on people's front lawns—maybe even backyards—as he goes to deliver their mail.

I wondered how many other beasts in the family—unknown ones who hid their taste for, say, live chickens or warm blood. Vampires, maybe, or ghouls, witches. It was a strange world out there beyond the glass.

At supper, my uncle read the newspaper or did the crossword puzzle, never looking at his food and seldom talking to the rest of us—that is Grandma, my younger sister, and me—except for "Pass the…" And, after each meal, my uncle would reach in his pocket, pull out a clean pressed handkerchief—one I had ironed—and honk away into it, setting all the glass to rattling.

Sometimes, following his after-dinner nap, my uncle would play blackjack with me, while my grandma and sister watched cowboys on television. My uncle would give me ten pennies, which he counted out in slow moves with his thumb and index finger, and he would try to teach me how to gamble.

Gambling had been the downfall of the family. My dead wastrel grandfather had blown the food money on the horses during the Depression, and my uncle had to quit school at age twelve and get a job to support his six brothers and sisters.

But the desire to gamble ran like a black seam through all of our natures, so my uncle deemed it his god-ordained task to teach me how to deal with it. "Set yourself a limit and don't go over it," he'd say as he dealt the cards. "Once you lose what you told yourself you could lose, walk away from the table." The wisdom here was mostly lost on me at age nine, since it took most of my effort just to add up the two cards and figure out if I should stick or ask for another one—and, most of all, how much I should bet.

I never won and he never let me win. That would not have prepared me for life, where nobody ever let you win anything. You had to scratch out everything you got on this godforsaken planet, he told me as he swept the pennies back into an old Mavrakos candy box that still held a faint aroma of chocolate covered cherries. When he replaced the lid, a whoosh of air escaped. The pennies were now sealed in a dark, airless place. Another lesson for me. Hang onto your money. You never knew when another Depression would hit. The world is a terrible place.

Yes, my uncle tried to prepare me for life. He gave me object lessons and the grizzled wisdom he'd gained from hard knocks. Each evening at the dining room table was another lesson, another day at life's school. I paid attention, and I remembered what he told me, and he liked that. But I didn't believe him for a minute, and I think he liked that even more. He wanted someone to prove him wrong—to make him believe there was something to hope for on this patch of dust.

Lesson over, he'd pick up the paperback mystery he kept tucked in his chair in the living room. It seemed that he read a new one every day. Books with the same glossy covers depicting long-legged women and men holding revolvers—only the titles changed. Life was a mystery to my uncle, and he absorbed himself in these novels night after night—perhaps the next one would solve the riddle of it all for him.

Life was a puzzle to Grandma. After she'd completed one of her jigsaws, she'd ponder it for a few days. The pieces had all been put together and there was the picture, and she'd gaze at it from close up or step back to get a long view. It was as if there was a secret message that she had to find, some answer. But, after a few days, she'd break up the pieces, one by one, and set them back in the box and shove the box onto the high shelf in the hallway closet. Then she'd send me out to the dime store the next day to buy another. Perhaps the next one. Maybe it would be there, what she was looking for.

I could see them from where I sat at the dining room table. He with the Mystery, and she with the Puzzle. Their heads bent, their glasses misted from the effort. A bus rolled down the street and the house shook. The glass rattled. We were still here, after all.

"Do you think the charms are ready yet?" I asked.

No reply from either the Mystery or the Puzzle.

"Is it time for the charms?" I said, throwing my voice from my room to theirs, like a ventriloquist breathing words into a doll.

They looked up. I had disturbed the Mystery, I had interrupted the Puzzle.

"Not yet," my uncle said. A bead of sweat fell from the end of his nose onto the mystery. He studied the page of his book. The circle of water widened until it filled the page, soaked through and glued all the pages together. No use pondering the Mystery any more tonight.

"Let's check," I said.

"We'll go when your sister can come along," he said, pointing to my sister asleep on the striped sofa.

"We'll bring her some back," I said. "I'll give her all the best ones."

He heaved himself up from his chair. Then he reached out and picked up the box of pennies and placed it under his arm. He motioned me to the front door with his head.

"Bring me back a..." my grandmother called.

We were going out. Outside. Out there. That place beyond the front door. My uncle was still wearing his house slippers, and I had on no shoes at all.

I skipped down the sloping sidewalk to the end of the block, while he scooted along behind. Dusk was almost on us: the cars at the curb, the people on the porches, the fading games of hopscotch, the grass, the flowers, the trees, all were lit with the glow of approaching sundown, like objects shining behind a glass.

We entered the dark cool cave of the corner candy store. I rant to the glass gumball machine and my uncle shuffled behind in his house shoes. We had been watching this gumball machine for weeks. My uncle wouldn't part of any of his precious chocolate-covered-cherry-smelling pennies until he could be sure that I'd get a charm along with the gum. We waited until enough people had put in their pennies, so that now the level of gumballs was almost down to the bottom and the charms were just about in reach.

I looked through the glass dome of the gumball machine and wanted everything inside: the tiny pink piano and the gold ring with the blue stone as big as a robin's egg. I wanted the little man in the brown derby. I wanted the ballerina and the Eiffel Tower and the Cinderella slipper and all the rest. Everything.

My uncle watched me wanting all these things. Then he opened his candy box and offered the pennies to me.

I grabbed a penny and slid it into the slot, then tried to turn the heavy metal lever. It was tight and hard to move, but my uncle didn't help me. That would not have been a good way to prepare me for life. He let me struggle until I turned it myself. I opened the metal latch. I had a black gumball and the gold ring.

My uncle held out the lid of his candy box, and I put them inside. We stood there, me struggling with the machine, him watching, until all the gumballs and all the charms were in the lid of his box. I put my nose up to the glass and looked inside. Nothing left. We had it all.

My uncle carried the box home under his arm. I walked at his side and listened to the gumballs and charms rolling around inside. Then I tried to remember what my grandmother had wanted us to bring her, but it was lost.

PART IX
OUTDOORS

DIANE EAGLE KATAOKA

Summer Haiku

This giant blue spruce
soars higher into the sky
lying here smelling sun

Electric Pass

Of all the steps taken on a hike—
parsing of altitudes
into thick aspen woods
stuttering switchbacks and
whistlepig scree—
I am fondest of those
that collapse us midway
in the shade of an ancient
blue spruce—delirious
sweaty punctuation between
stacks of verse.

Pause, inhale sweet pine scent,
cool respite from intense vertical summer,
strike up through open meadows of
melting snowfields toward gothic
slate peaks rimming the sky
at the summit—
mountain crests and hollows
spread in purpled shadows
beneath us like a many-tiered skirt.

DIANE EAGLE KATAOKA

Fauré Fourhands

Just now, leaning my head back
to catch the laze of sun
in aspen leaves,
I am pulled into the sound
of Fauré fourhands coming
from the music tent.

Lines of my life
converge
in harmony so vivid
caused by this sun
no doubt and
the piano notes
clustered in glorious
patterns not seen since
going to sleep stoned
and running movies
on the backs of my eyelids.

IVON PREFONTAINE

Paintbrush

God paints the world—
Gentle touches;
Full strokes;
Vivid blends;
Vibrant colours give life
By summer's path, grows
Nature's tool.

LARRY D. THOMAS

The Night We Were Gods

They hung by thread
just above our heads
in the entryway,
five hummingbirds
of clear red glass

covered with glitter.
Absentmindedly,
we brushed them
with the tips
of our forefingers,

rubbed our eyelids
and smeared them
with galaxies
of tiny stars.
For several hours,

till we showered,
and never even
noticing, we blessed
everything we touched
with crushed light.

From *Larry D. Thomas: New and Selected Poems* (TCU Press, 2008)

LARRY D. THOMAS

Apricots

A few blocks off the plaza,
in the Santa Fe evening light
the color of brandy,
on the street below the branches

of the tree, they glowed in rosy,
yellow hues as if a god
had ripped the sundown, rolled it
into fuzzy, dimpled balls,

and flung them to the ground.
Fast as we could, deep
into the fabric of our shorts,
we crammed them till our pockets

sagged, and lumbered down
the darkening street
like lumpy angels, holy
with the light of apricots.

From *Larry D. Thomas: New and Selected Poems* (TCU Press, 2008)

LARRY D. THOMAS

Hopscotch

Standing in line
in their bright sundresses,
they make a perfect spectrum.

One at a time they hop,
flopping their pigtails,
touching their upper lips

with their pointed tongues.
The figure on which they hop
is laid out in the shape

of a door today at least
they could care less
what it opens to,

each taking her hops in order,
picking up the stone
sans a bobble.

DANIEL MCGINN

Remembering the Taste of a Blackberry I Ate Last Summer

For my grandfather, whose name I can't remember

I think it took less than a handful of seeds strategically dropped at the side of the creek that roams through the backyard behind my house on Willow Street to create these bramble bushes that arch and dive every which way, weaving leaves and thorns into nature's rebellious unkempt hedges.

It might have been bear shit or it could have been deer shit that brought this gift to my back door, back before there was a back door, or a house, or a road was carved out and paved between the weeping willows. I wish I could have been there.

It's early spring but soon flowers will start to appear. Later I will watch as the flowers disappear. I will ask myself, *Where have all the flowers gone?* It takes a while for a blackberry to mature. God teaches patience to all of us who love blackberries and can't wait to eat them.

A flower hatches a green berry, which becomes a pink berry that turns into a red berry and then the berry turns black: a cluster of niblets, a gathering of fruit bubbles. It's a pretty complicated process.

There was this one blackberry I ate when I was berry picking last summer. My mouth remembers it like it was only yesterday. I picked this berry and balanced it between my upper and lower front teeth. I closed my lips over its bubbles and bit down slowly. The flavors escaped their bubble skins. The first thing that popped into my mouth was the taste of pepper, which was quickly followed by the distinct burst of bazooka gum mingled with barbershop bay rum. I closed my eyes and the smoky tang of cherry tobacco bit me at the back of the tongue—this was the blackberry I had been searching for. Never before had a blackberry rimmed my eyes with Grandpa tears.

My father introduced me to my grandpa, who didn't like to speak if he wasn't getting paid for it. He was a salesman. He had to speak to make a living. If Grandpa wasn't smoking his pipe, he was filling it. Little flecks of tobacco would float from his shirt pocket as he bent down to pick me up. He used to call me Pat or Bill but he seldom remembered my name. That seems fair. I don't remember that much about him.

Grandpa was buried in his favorite suit with bits of cherry tobacco hidden in the lining of his coat and trouser cuffs. If they hadn't buried him in that coffin, we might have had cherry tobacco leaves growing in the hills of California. Grandpa would have liked that.

The funeral was held in an old stained glass Catholic church filled with incense, candles, and Latin prayers. Holy Communion was served to the mourners who were simultaneously sad and serious.

My dad, my mom, and all six kids dressed in black. We opened and closed all of the doors of the family station wagon that served as the pace car for the funeral procession. Everyone started their engines and we followed the coffin up the road to the cemetery.

Halfway up the hill, Dad, Mom, and all six kids started laughing like a bunch of manic depressives who had given away their medicine a long time ago. Once we got started laughing, we just couldn't stop.

Here's how the story goes: they took away Grandpa's driver's license. These finger-waggers told him he could no longer drive a motor vehicle. Grandpa bought a golf cart because it ran on a battery instead of a motor and it was sort of street-legal. He drove off in his electric vehicle, rising up the narrow road that ran behind the golf course, figuring he could get to the market by taking the scenic route. Seeing that the sun was shining was occasion enough to start filling his pipe as the golf cart slowly weaved its way up the steep hill. His golf cart veered to the edge of the asphalt and began to tip like the world's smallest SUV. Grandpa rolled down the hill and died in the thorny arms of blackberry bushes.

The generations that followed Grandpa were not afraid to be seen laughing at his life as they drove toward his grave in a funeral procession.

PAUL FERICANO

The Day I Almost Died

It was at a family picnic
on a perfect Sunday afternoon in summer.
I was three years old.

My father, grilling steaks
dropped a juicy one, slipped from his fork
and landed in the dirt near his feet.

Cursing the dead cow that gave its life
he flung it under a nearby sycamore
where hungry yellow jackets swarmed.

I only saw the dazzle that day:
a glistening pulsating color of golden light
within my reach and easy to touch.

I remember the stings, trying to breathe
and the panic in my father's eyes
as he scooped me up, frantic

and dunked me in a nearby creek,
smearing my small swollen body, limp
with cold bottom mud.

At the hospital they praised him,
told him his quick thinking saved my life.
He nodded, covered his face and cried.

Bees

Wise bees will tell you:
"Natura in minima
Maxima"—kindly

Translating it
As "Nature is the greatest
In the smallest things."

Bees' making life sweet
Made man's harsh evolution
More tolerable.

Almost each mouthful
Of food owes its existence to
Pollinating bees.

It's been said, "If bees
Disappear, man has only
A few years to live."

Bees are eusocial—
Meaning their life is ordered
For the benefit

Of everyone in
The hive: construction workers,
Nurses, guards, grocers,

Housekeepers,
Foragers, and gigolos
And undertakers.

Man's society
Is largely anti-social.
A kleptocracy.

Man, who steals from bees,
Repays them with pesticide
Yet they dance to work.
Emma Goldman said
That all revolutions should
Involve dancing, but

No revolution
Has produced anything
As good as bees

And Tolstoy believed
They'd devised the ideal
Society for man.

No society
Has a talisman with the
Power of honey.

One ounce of honey
Enables a bee to fly
Round the whole world.

If bees' stamina
Is scaled up to human level,
Man is quite outclassed.

A bee beats its wings
Over eleven thousand
Times in a minute.

Its brain's a cubic
Millimetre whose wiring
Beats silicon chips.

A bee, said Karl Marx,
Can "put architects to shame
In constructing cells."

The bee's venom is
The most powerful substance
In the natural world.

Bee acupuncture
Can extend man's lifespan by
Curing arthritis.

A bee's venom can
Open up neural pathways,
Following a stroke.
➢

Honey can dress wounds—
Since microbes can't live in it,
It's antiseptic.

Alexander the
Great was embalmed in honey
And lasted decades.

In Ephesus bees
Would symbolize Artemis,
And stood for wisdom.

So Pythagoras, Achilles
And Plato were fed honey
In their infancy.

The "gift of heaven"
Virgil called it and,
In his Georgics,

He said it conveyed
Prescience; and the priestess
At Delphi was called

The 'Delphic Bee' as
Her powers were oracular:
She saw the future.

Before Chernobyl
Was understood, bees
Wisely stayed in their hives.

The priest Jonathan,
In *1 Samuel 14,*
Would take some honey

From a honey-comb
Then, "as his hand met his mouth,
His eyes were enlightened."
The letters in the
Poet Deborah's Hebrew name,
Dbr, means bee;

It also means truth—
Both being on a mission
To improve the world

With sweetness and light—
For if reason's sweet
Why pull a sour face?

Bees have made honey
For 150 million years
And the Pyramids,

When rediscovered,
Showed that honey had been placed
Near Pharoah's body—

An immortal food
Which still tasted good after
Five thousand years.

Bees defend themselves
Without paying someone else
To do it for them.

Bees' flower power
Is not a drug-enhanced dream:
Their flying's for real.

'Where the bee sucks there
Suck I, in a cowslip's bell
I lie.' *Paradise!*

The buzzing of bees
Indicating contentment
Is archetypal:

The soundtrack to the
Land of milk and honey, man's
Sustaining ideal.
Each bee has five eyes.
Mystics reckon a third eye
Bestows occult powers.

Five eyes could give you
The ability to see
Some things that man can't.

Raymond King Shurtz

Buffalo Heading North

I could not rise today.

I felt so good the day before, so good
I even climbed the mountain!
I was manifesting foolish youth
striking stars with sticks
laughing like Butch and Sundance
pulling iron on old bones
roping mesquites with simple ease
carrying the bottle of lightning
in my pocket I took from storms long ago…

I was a buffalo then—
the truth is in the story my friend,
and stories are never free.

Why just ten years ago,
I climbed and leaped like my brother
the fleet-footed gazelle
taking me easily to the top!
The wind had cleared! Sky nary a cloud!
I looked to the The North!
The North! And Summer!
Where the grass is thick!
Where the Henry Mountains loom like
horses of giant Paiutes riding for the hunting grounds!

But, alas, I have walked in too many snows.
There was the three days stuck in barbed wire
the deep hole I didn't see—
the twist to free myself—
the showdown with Gorr of the Canadian herd
another blow to the leg and shoulder—
Then, the fire, Oh, the fire!

This morning did I sleep?
Did I dream?
Pain shot down my leg
Like the jack I wanted
to throw back to my dry throat
chasing it with the cold spring water
of my wild days on trails

to lessen its fire
make me forget the human part of me
burning going down—
ancient firewater, yes, dreams.

It was the last trip North
I faced the stumble
the withering of flesh
Oh, God! There it is!
the gradual limp of doom.

The eyes of
my comrades gradually
begin to look away—
retreating from the
flame that once
burned from within my spirit.
"Sorrow, my oh my brother!"
"We know the fear,
we will do what it can."
"We cannot make
promises though!"
"Shall we hold vigilance
this winter?"
"Shall we buy you some time
in wooded thickets?"

Maybe I'll head to
The summer pastures—
the great Navajo Mountain
find some cool mud
In some thorny thicket
smile and tell stories
of a hundred moons
to the young ones—
maybe one or two more seasons
with luck—
with random notes
that nature will soon beg to write

Pain is not a cover
Pain is not a lover
Pain is a price—
A life lived too long
As a reckless young buffalo—
The wolf does not care for my stories,
➢

for my pain
for my future
he will relieve
My suffering with
a short bite to my neck
it could be worse…
It could be worse.

RUTH MOON KEMPHER

Queen Anne's Lace

My Gramma knew the names of all the field
flowers, but I didn't always listen. The lavender
lilac was French, she said, which I knew was far off
where there was war, which wasn't fitting. Peace—
there were Peace roses in her garden, and Ramblers—
that made sense somehow, since everybody went out
somewhere, but could come home. Three-Star flag
in her window for three boys, one was for my Dad—
Lily-of-the-Valley and Mock Orange by the porch.
Too long in the south now, where it hardly
grows anything without stickers or violent smell
my favorites were Queen Anne's Lace and
Dutchman's Breeches, sometimes called, if I
remember rightly, Butter and Eggs, in lots miscalled
"vacant," where grasses congregate—bugs
and milkweed pods, oozing moths and butterflies—
the moths that drift, white over dry rows of pea vines
like early snow. Summer was the best time, then.
        Carrot smell, vague, of Queen Anne's lace
embroidered my days, easy. Looking up under
its umbrella, kaleidoscope curds, white knurls
on green spokes, turned slowly—Summer
was for hiding then, mostly, looking up.

First published in *5 A.M.*

GERALD LOCKLIN

The Winter Trees of Summer
For the Irishman Joyce and the Welshman Thomas

On Radnor Avenue, one block away,
The trees have not forgotten the unforeseeable frost,
Although the days at least at last are warming.
The municipal arborists arbitrarily decreed that this year
A severe trim was in order all the way up to
Their willowy, widowy peaks,
Reducing their Wagnerian tufts to Mozartian muppets
That used to bend as shady canopy, arcade, chapel or
Bishop's arch-nave the length of the thoroughfare,
Within our tract, like baobabs or jacarandas,
Though my wife insists they are not either,
Are a species with which she is not familiar,
Maybe gardened by the Brothers Grimm.
Their branches now, thick as anacondas,
Dance their horizontal, giant, yogurt-yaugust,
Almost oaken, salamander-gray-great-graynesses
That bear not fruit or nuts or bombast,
Just the threat of nightmarish, Ovidian,
Asphyxiating, beddy-bye, annihilating hugs
To cars, homes, women, children, pets, planets
And would-be SuperDuperHeroes. Our leaders tried to play
Dum-dum-Dalilas to their Samsonite Thuggage,
While taxes, Abraxas, and Iran distracted us.
They will limply drop us down the limpid walls of wells
Of pothole loneliness into Hell's Lethean, oblisionary
Looping Lena's Leap.

JACKIE PLEDGER-SKWERSKI

Green

It was summer and everything was green. Once settled with her newborn son in her hospital room, Ivy could rest and think of what she wanted to name him. It was her choice. The father had left town when she'd told him she was pregnant. And of course she didn't want to involve her parents. What could she name him that was unique but simple. Green, of course!

From her window at the hospital, she could see the river, the bright green willow trees, and the redwood trees in the distance. How she loved them. Tall, some in the area were close to two hundred and fifty feet tall and had been estimated to up to two thousand years old.

When the doctor said she could go home, Ivy called her mother, Mauve, who picked her up in her new red Mercedes. There was no car seat for the baby, but Ivy made do by sitting in the back with the seatbelt around both of them.

"Why didn't you come to see us?" asked Ivy, once they were moving.

"Ivy, you didn't even tell me you were going to the hospital," Mauve scolded. " How could I even know he'd been born?"

"Mom, get over in the right lane. I live in Arcata, now. I don't want to go to Eureka," Ivy said.

Arcata and Eureka were twin cities on the rugged northern California coast. At one time, Eureka had been the home of lumber barons and an affluent city. Arcata was a college town, populated by students and nature-loving young people drawn to the area's environmental causes.

"I was taking you to Eureka because Dad and I can take better care of you away from all those Humboldt University types. That's how you got pregnant in the first place."

"Mom, I'm capable of taking care of myself. I want to go back to my own house. I'm more comfortable there. I know people. Everybody in Arcata isn't a hippy. Please don't make me go back to Eureka," Ivy pleaded.

"Wish granted," said Mauve, changing lanes so fast she just missed hitting another car. "Why you want to live in that little hovel way out in a cow pasture, I don't know. And I ought to be flogged for letting a seventeen-year-old live like that."

"I want to live like that."

To change the subject, Mauve asked: "What did you name the baby?"

"Green," Ivy replied. "Green Jacoby."

"We don't have anybody in the family with a name like that," said Mauve. "Why didn't you name him something like Franklin, or Bradford, or even Charles? And where did that name, Jacoby come from? What's wrong with our last name?"

"The people at the hospital told me that legally, every baby has to carry its father's name," Ivy said. "And whether Mark Jacoby stuck around after I told him he was going to be a father doesn't matter. Green is my son and I'm going to raise him."

∞

As he grew up Green enjoyed hiking and riding his bicycle through the forest. He and his friends also liked to play Frisbee there. It was especially fun in the redwoods because the huge trees form obstacles making the game more challenging.

His almost spiritual love of the redwoods began when his high school took the seniors on a trip to Muir Woods, near San Francisco. When Green wandered into the woods alone, he found himself breathing the deliciously moist, pine-scented air and marveled at the majesty of these magnificent giants.

"How come they can grow so tall?" Green asked one of the national park rangers.

"Climate," the ranger told him. "Northern California is an ideal place for them because we have chilly winters, pleasantly warm summers and just the right amount of moisture for the trees to thrive. The ocean creates lots of fog in the mountains and of course it rains a lot in winter."

An excellent student Green won a full scholarship to Humboldt State University, where he met other students interested in saving the redwoods. Of course Green knew about the protests and remembered the time when the students climbed into the redwoods nearest the university and lived in them, leaving only to go to class. The locals called the encampment "Ewok village," naming it after the Star Wars tree dwellers.

Green knew that a local logging company was allowed to cut the redwoods in certain predetermined areas. But what upset Green and others was the fact that the company cut trees in areas where they were forbidden to log, removing trees in large swaths down the side of a mountain leaving the slopes bare, brown and lifeless. Rainstorms caused mudslides down the sides of the mountains, swallowing villages and homes.

Green had never participated in a protest. He now felt called to join in. He made it his goal to do his part to help save the environment. In a forestry ecology class one day, the professor mentioned that despite the fact that the university didn't encourage student protests, tree sitting had brought about some positive changes. It was no longer necessary for people to sit in trees to prevent clear cutting. The local logging company had sold to another firm and the new administration understood woodland ecology and was willing to negotiate. He attributed their success to the efforts of a girl named Julia Butterfly Hill, who sat in a tree for two years.

⟨⟨⟩⟩

One evening when Green was watching the news on television, the reporter mentioned that a new logging company had begun clear cutting in the Grizzly Bear Creek and Six Rivers area.

Green called the group that was behind the Headwaters tree sit. Yes, they were sponsoring this protest and needed people to sit in trees.

"Bring a sleeping bag, some changes of shirts and jeans, a flashlight with extra batteries, a tarp if you have one, and anything else you think you might need," the girl who answered the phone said. "This won't be a long tree sit, but you need to be comfortable up there. And don't worry, there will be someone else with you in the tree."

After a two-hour drive, he arrived and met the other tree sitters. "I'm a little new at this, so you'll have to coach me along the way," he said. "Sorry, I didn't have a tarp."

"We've got several," one of the men said. "This is the tree."

Green looked up in awe. Beautiful and old growth, meaning that no part of it had ever been cut.

The trunk went up forty-five feet before any branches appeared. Then branch after branch sprang from the mother tree creating little trees of its own.

"First you're going to have to pick out a nature name, not to be cute but to protect your real identity should we all get arrested. Some of the people have picked out names like Spruce, Almond, and I use the name "Nut.""

"How about 'Leaf?' My real name is Green."

"Well, folks, this is Leaf, and his real name is Green," the young man announced to the other protesters.

"Does that sound like a tree lover? You bet it does. Now let's get started."

Tree sitters live on six by six square platforms in the branches and have a support team of four or five who visit every couple of days. They bring food and survival supplies, which they hoist up with ropes, and they take away their waste in big plastic garbage bags. They sleep in sleeping bags because they live as high as two hundred feet off the ground and the weather at that height can get very damp, cold and windy. A tarp is hung on one side to block the wind. They cook on propane stoves.

"It's not all fun and games," the young man warned. "Many a tree sitter gets hurt doing this. A young man named Gypsy was killed when a logger deliberately cut down a tree so that it would fall on him. He died and they named the mountain for him, Gypsy Mountain. A girl got her pelvis shattered when a pipe bomb exploded in her car. Another girl died when the tree she was sitting in was shaken hard by hostile loggers."

"To get up into the trees we wear harnesses with a strong rope attached and to the tree and we hoist ourselves a foot at a time," Nut explained. "We wear extra ropes clipped to the harness so that when get to the end of one, we toss another one over a strong branch above us and continue climbing. Getting down is much faster."

Green buckled on the harness and started his ascent. The protesters crowded beneath him to cheer him on and to catch him if he fell.

"You're doing great, Leaf, keep climbing," yelled Nut.

"You're a real trooper," a girl called to him

It took Green almost two hours to climb the one hundred and fifty feet to his platform and when he got there he was both exhausted and elated. Catching a breath, he stood up tall on the platform, stretched his arms out wide and cried, "I can fly, just like Julie Butterfly! And as long as I stay up here, the loggers can't touch this tree."

Tamara Madison

Strawberries

Fragole, fresas, klubniki, fraises—
is there a term that names them better
than *strawberry?* I think of sunshine
and straw hats, picnics, boating parties,
a barber shop quartet, homemade
ice cream, grainy and sweet, everything

warm, wholesome, innocent, old fashioned.
Near my house there's a strawberry field
that begins its work in spring, the stray seeds
emerging unbidden in neighboring gardens,
on walkways, from cracks in the sidewalk,
the clean white petals yielding pale-green

hearts that swell, redden, and fill
with so much happiness to give in their sweet-tart
flesh, the fertile seeds that linger in your teeth
and remind you of a gentle time only moments
ago when you tasted the essence of summer
on your grateful tongue.

BRUCE WEIGL

Pastoral as Complaint

      The robin is so quarrelsome. He barks to no one in the trees;
he fluffs his body twice its size and rattles in the leaves.
      He doesn't know or won't accept the nest is empty now,
The eggs a tatter on the ground. The storm was quick,
      we didn't see it come; no sound above the hum.

a summer morning makes when god is in his place
      and we are free of tragedies that pile up along the way.
The robin is so quarrelsome;
      he thinks his life is gone just like the nest,
but he's like the rest of us, it's only just begun.

SUSIE SWEETLAND GARAY

Ripening

The things our
bodies do are
quite miraculous
she tells me.

I went to the
doctor expecting
a stern face
and a lecture.
To be told to wait.
To keep trying.
To be patient.

But instead she listens,
not only to the facts of it,
but she lets me tell
the feel of it too.

The relief is immense
and hope comes in
on the room's current.

Right now her body is
building a placenta
and a face.
No wonder she is
so tired
she says.

I learned in my
first marriage
to be an
excellent liar,
which is sometimes
a very useful skill.

A berry hangs there
in the sun
ripening
slowly.
I taste the sweetness before
it gets to my mouth.

TATE SWINDELL

Conception of Love
        for Leslie Winer

Remember when we were younger
When it was acceptable
to lie down on the sidewalk
Our cheeks
                pressed against
the melting
                summer cement

The scent
of chrysanthemums
and honeysuckle
clinging to our clothes

Anxiety of deadlines
nowhere to be found
Until the sun set for the night
signaling our curfew

Slowly walking home
Holding dirty hands
with sweaty palms
Trying to extend the magic hour

Holes in jeans
and skinned knees
Band-aids worn like badges
Embracing our crutches
Crying just because

Death, a stranger
we weren't allowed to speak to

Those moments
when my eyes
would catch your eyes
Lingering
Wondering
Who would be
the first to laugh

The edges of your smile
began to rise
And I knew
        ➢

I knew
that you could hear
this heart beating
through my cheek
as it melted
the summer sidewalk

MERRILL FARNSWORTH

Shameless

Summer is a crazed riot
Of jungle green, cherry red
And high noon yellow
Primal heat seeking ripeness
No holding back, no rain checks
No second chances.

PART X
TRAVELS

CLIFTON SNIDER

Taos, New Mexico

The movie runs all summer.
The toilet in the men's room
leaks over the floor. You see your neighbor
at the post office and the Safeway store.
Like the Indian pots, outsiders deck the paseo,
the shops, the galleries. Fifteen-year-old girls
smoke pot on the plaza at night. Low-riders yell,
"Lookin' good, girl." State police circle
the square. The bar closes at midnight.
Gray-headed flower children
tread the streets.
                              Blood relatives
chatter, swarm, caress like cottonwood seeds,
puffballs filling cracks in the street.

Rain drops little spider feet,
tracks on your car.
                              Dust-laden air
spreads like paint on a canvas.

I stare at the *Sangre de Cristos*,
vigas, mud houses: *la vida*,
the reaches of light.

                    (1984)

From *Moonman: New and Selected Poems* (World Parade Books, 2012)

CLIFTON SNIDER

Indian Summer in New Mexico

The high desert sky
nearly cloudless
the day before the clocks fall back,
sun bright as an atomic flash,
cottonwoods, aspens, maple, willows—
leaves falling like they never do
back home in Southern California,
a day to walk on roads
whose dust rises with every pickup
& Prius that passes,
& as you watch a northern flicker
with red mustache
perch on a slender stump
two dogs cross the field
and the creek bed
and join you on the road—
you shoo them off
& happily they scamper away
& you walk down a quiet residential street,
one house a junk yard of old cars & trucks
stuffed with all shapes of rusted metal & tubes,
further up a majestic modern adobe,
unoccupied for the season,
kids jump on a trampoline in another yard
while grandma and grandpa sit in the shade—
then back to your *casita* & for once
you leave the door open.

—6 November 2010
Taos, New Mexico

From *Moonman: New and Selected Poems* (World Parade Books, 2012)

BART PLANTENGA

Summer Mid-Manhattan

Excerpt from the novel *Beer Mystic*

Walking home via Rudy's, a real place somewhere between Heaven and Hell, its authenticity threatened by developers and those who crave the comforts that the simulation of actuality offer. The problem isn't finding your way out of yourself but where it all wandered off to. Hell, I can't even convince myself I know a way out of here—Rudy's, a labyrinth of reasonably priced pitchers of beer that fuel conversations edging on madness, the shriveled wieners turning on the electric spit, Broadway vets in week-old pancake makeup, sagging knee-worn spandex, writers in suspiciously threadbare suits toting paperbacks they may or may not have written, crumpled fedoras, happy flatulence amplified by balding, wobbly bar stools, and a juke full of high sentiments.

You can have great conversation here if you got the lungs. Wear your galoshes if you plan to use the toilets. As I enter, I hear the tail-end of "Walk Like An Egyptian," which segues into "I Knew You Were Waiting For Me" [Aretha Franklin and George Michael], which I, to my horror, know some of the lyrics to, and am singing along to along with about twenty other patrons [this is as close as you get to strangers!], as I spot Mike G., *conspiratoriologist extraordinaire*, Martin Luther King assassination buff and poet of the paranoid. This is synchronicity: the fact that my ex-boss Lee Morgan, who I just exchanged farewells with uptown, lived on 125th [aka Martin Luther King Boulevard] and Mike's preoccupations with MLK, conspiracies and on how they infiltrate every aspect of our lives including mixed drinks [black and white: Kahlua and milk; black and tan: a pale ale plus a stout]. He is not about to move from his stool once he's in Rudy's; do that and you lose your stool and your proximity to the bartender. Rumor has it that Mike wears a basic urine drainage bag of Malaysian manufacture to ensure his possession of his favorite stool between the wiener warmer and the jukebox. He does let me share his pitcher of Pabst Blue Ribbon—save the glass, I'm thirsty, I'll just drink right from the pitcher.

"I'm weeding through *MEMPHIS, TEN*," he yells through the music, lovingly wiping the beer foam mustache from my upper lip with the sleeve of a coat that hasn't been washed since 1966. Trying to solve the problem of the book's smugness as truth wrapped around a novel.

"I know too much. The book reveals too much to ever be published. Ten spent shells. People not already dead may die. A dossier of death threats. Brilliance is what they all fear."

"Whose this 'they'?"

"Ah, I keep pounding the phone lines until I get toxed, man, really toxed, then roll over until I recover and start pounding again. But if I don't get the novel out next year—on the whatever anniversary of the assassination—that's that. I go back to selling encyclopedias door to door. I know it's a long shot, but..."

Tom T. Hall was now singing—where else had I recently heard this song? In Sally's? In the Po-Mo? WFMU?—in my head?: "Roll out the barrel / And lend me your ears / I like beer / It makes me a jolly good fellow / I like beer / It helps me unwind / And sometimes makes me feel mellow..." We sing along, others join us—the accuracy of the lyrics is not essential. We vow to get together, knowing very well that we want to but seldom do. Some hearty and meaningful backslaps as he hands me a beer coaster upon which he has scrawled: SHORT NECK—O, MEDIOCRE GIANT—DIES UNWED— GENES WITHER—THE GOVERNMENT DID IT AND IT IS US. DON'T OVER-ESTIMATE THE POWER OF CONSCIOUSNESS AND UNDERESTIMATE THE POWER OF UNCONSCIOUS OR INVOLUNTARY PROCESSES.

Mike G. continued to sit where he always sits at that gnawed corner of the bar, saying the things he always said, that always sounded like foreboding or an aphorism, things that wafted about in the air like the heavenly scent of flapjacks in cartoons starring hungry chipmunks. Anyone was free to ignore him or quote him.

"Me, I only drink to keep from getting depressed about how depressing it is when I'm not drinking."

"OK."

"But drinking gets you depressed when you realize it's only drinking that prevents the onset of the depression of sobriety."

"You got me goin' in circles."

"Maybe it's Kepler or a song by Blackfoot."

Someone overheard us and responded by letting out a replica of the little "woo" that Lee Michaels punctuates his one hit "Do You Know What I Mean" with.

"I get depressed just thinkin' about how much I drink."

"Have a drink, it'll make you forget."

"But my liver's there to remind me. And I just get depressed when I think of what my liver has to go through for the sake of my soul."

"Like a cleaning lady in the service of a banker."

"I don't wanna think about it. Gimme a drink. I'm gettin' depressed."

"You could just slash your wrists."

"Or have another drink," he nods. And then nods off comfortably as if Rudy's is his living room and the light from the juke is like the setting sun.

I wander out and walk further downtown. Mike meant what he said, he did, really did; it's no one's fault that opportunity does not knock. Because, point is, although Lee bought the night's rounds [Belgian beers: chosen by name and reputation—Folie, Piraat, La Moraal— beers so obscure and strange, they were almost revolutionary] and, although he shook my hand forcefully as if he did not want to let go, we never did keep in touch. Even though the Lexington Avenue line backbones its way up from my hood to his on 125th, near where Langston Hughes lived. On the going away card—an image of a pirate drinking beer—which I read only outside, he had written: "The night is beautiful, / So the faces of *my people*." It's only later that Nice informs me it's from a famous Langston Hughes poem.

In any case, there is something in how we all get bounced around the city, which keeps us from staying in touch. Where you quickly wander off the path of good intentions lost in a labyrinth of diversions of escalating distraction.

When I got "home," I was greeted on our front stoop by a strange Rorschach puke splotch in the shape of a guitar warmed to a hard pancake by the heat of our streets and stoops. Somebody had stuck an hors d'oeuvre toothpick with an I LOVE NY flag into the mess. The droll gesture is one of eternal hope, of catastrophe overcome.

THOMAS R. THOMAS

Palm Springs

We would get the house in Palm Springs
in the off season when
no one else wanted it.

I was thirteen and
I was good company
for Mom and Dad so they
could spend their time alone.

I spent the whole day
playing scuba diver
in the pool, then dash
to the house dancing
in front of the sliding
glass door until I
could pop inside.

Late in the day I
walked the streets,
scanning the desert
with the wind in my face.

Floating in the still pool
with the water licking my face
I stare at the sparkling stars.

PAUL LAURENCE DUNBAR

Summer in the South

The oriole sings in the greening grove
    As if he were halfway waiting,
The rosebuds peep from their hoods of green,
    Timid, and hesitating.
The rain comes down in a torrent sweep
    And the nights smell warm and pinety,
The garden thrives, but the tender shoots
    Are yellow-green and tiny.
Then a flash of sun on a waiting hill,
    Streams laugh that erst were quiet,
The sky smiles down with a dazzling blue
    And the woods run mad with riot.

EDDIE WOODS

Retour New York-Amsterdam

I sometimes think when summer rolls round
here in Amsterdam, how nice it might be
to suddenly find myself in New York.
But just for a day, mind you,
or perhaps overnight.

Stroll about in Greenwich Village;
quaff an espresso at the Rienzi
(or isn't it waiting anymore,
on MacDougal Street?);
play some chess
in Washington Square;
saunter by to Waverly Place,
book a room at what back then
was still known as the Hotel Earle
(I always preferred it to the Chelsea...
which nonetheless would be my next stop,
as I headed on up into the swirl of midtown,
for a respectful visit with its artistic grandees).

Yeah, midtown Manhattan
to do the 'Broadway boogie'
all along the Great White Way
(it's really only true New Yorkers
who can wiggle quickly thru a crowd!).
Check out Times Square and Hell's Kitchen:
any black-beauty whores roaming the avenues,
or lingering in musty shadows as evening descends?
Hey, Central Park is also beckoning; and after that
my once beloved nor ever to be forgotten Harlem.

Indeed it would be nice. Providing of course
I didn't have to fly over! Could instead
snap my fingers and there I am,
sci-fi beamed to the Big Apple.
No airport check-in hassles,
no six or so hours without a fag,
no jumbo jets I can no longer stand
(give me the old Caravelles anytime).

So dig, best to simply leave it be. An occasional reverie,
between penning poems and burning the late-night oil away
as a native alien in Amsterdam. No 'retour' to New York for me.

Amsterdam, May 2009

Big Bear Vacation

We've become bird watchers
on the balcony
of the cabin at Big Bear Lake
observing bluejays flying down
to the porch railing
to feed on birdseed.
My husband, a man
who has worked more hours
than anyone I know,
every now and then rises
from the recliner to place
peanuts on the banister.
He's delighted when a bird
arrives, fills its beak,
then returns to the trees.
Today our family took off
to find excitement
at the Alpine slide,
and to check out info
about ziplining over ski trails
while we sit and gaze
at woods from the porch.
This man, who lived
on Hudson Boulevard,
a busy bus route
to New York City,
is now captivated by the view.
He acts like a little kid
when he spots a chipmunk,
squirrel, or rabbit.
It's a first in our married life
that he's taking time
to relax for hours
scanning trees for wild life.
My eyes follow the line
of the ski lift
to its mountain ridge,
bordered with pine trees
so knit together
that the tops of their branches
look like outstretched arms
praising the blue sky.

CAROLYN MILLER

Sunday Market in Pollensa

When I come around the corner, I see the pig legs,
dried and shrunken, laid out on the table, complete
with cloven hooves. An old man in a gray smock
cuts one into long thin slices, dark red
and laced with fat. I smell the salt cod
before I see it, stacked in brittle, fumey piles, next to
the olives, drenched in pools of brine. Then
a wide space filled with overflowing tables where
green garlic wilts in sheaves, the undulating bodies
of red peppers gleam, lettuces open like great
ragged flowers. One more time I am surprised by summer,
how suddenly it arrives with its mounds of bleeding berries,
so ripe, so dense with sweetness.

PART XI
AUGUST

JEFFREY C. ALFIER

Late Summer at Café Catalonia

I enter, and as the door slams behind
me, last night's wine bargains harsh with my skull.
With essential charm a waitress spies me:
"Good morning—anywhere you like," she says.
Truckers know that greeting like a safehouse.
With both her hands full of greasy dishes,
she carries a menu under her arm,
drops it on my table as she whisks by,
leaving a whiff of sweat, stale cigarettes
fused to cheap perfume, and disappointment.
She shouts hello to a man named Sundog.
Isn't this the place he'll always return,
his sad eyes saying he's permanent here?

This café is ruled by matrons like her—
all late middle-age, as if they'd been hired
from a class reunion, the year hushed-up.
To a lone man who stands to leave, one says,
"No Beth today?" As she adjusts his warped
table, his reply is murmured bitter
while ranchers gab to her on what plagues them
in the field: worn gears, wind, terminal rust.
Her cook stays invisible. He's rumored
a fugitive paid under the table.
All that means is he's one of us at heart,
each life worn as fence posts, but welcomed here,
like letters we wrote but never sent home.

win harms

summer solitude

do you remember the quiet solitude
of a warm august night
the smell of sage drifting through the air
as the sister sun bids the earth good night
leaving us with dreams of tomorrow?
do you remember the sweet serenity
of a final summer song
with the sound of stars laughing in harmony
as the mother moon awakens in peace
to share a piece of heaven?
i do.

Rubbed Out

Following intense and often bitter debate involving town officials and local citizenry, the construction of the new Wal-Mart was approved by the slimmest of margins. The long-abandoned Gardner farm at the north end of Granby, New Hampshire, was to be the site of the giant box store. The house that stood in the overgrown field was so decrepit that it took only one push by a backhoe to make it collapse. In no time, everything but a small patch of dense foliage at the far edge of the property was cleared so construction could begin.

Things were going according to plan until several centuries-old tombstones were discovered within that thicket. Work was immediately halted while the state historic society conducted an investigation. Rubbings of the stones were taken and while there were no dates on the actual granite slabs, a date did appear in the lower corner of all six of the paper impressions—one that was three months in the future, *August 11, 2012.*

"Okay, let's do it again," said Corey Glenn to his assistant, Fran Kramer. "This didn't just happen, right?"

Again, the mysterious date appeared on the rubbings heightening the bafflement of the historical society's field researchers.

"This is really weird," observed Fran, staring in disbelief at the numbers on the rice paper.

"Weird? No, this is just plain freaky," replied Corwin. "Shoot me doing a rubbing with your cell. We need to document this or nobody is going to believe us."

When Corwin finished, both he and Fran reviewed the recording several times.

"Pictures don't lie. Damned if we didn't just experience a paranormal event, or whatever they call it."

"Whoa, this *is* really spooky," responded Fran, her eyes darting from the cell phone screen to the headstones.

"Now what?"

"We'll take everything back to the office and see what Billings has to say," answered Corwin, rolling up the rubbings. "Let's record this one more time to make sure we have it, okay? This time you do the rubbing, and I'll play cameraman."

✄

Back in Manchester, the director of the historical society, Lionel Billings, was as perplexed by the inexplicable event as were his two preservationists. Since their return to the office, the legal representatives of the box store chain had called demanding to know when construction could resume. Reluctantly Billings attempted to explain why further inquiry needed to be conducted at the site, but his words were met with skepticism, and the society was accused of deliberately delaying the project.

"C'mon. We got forty men on payroll and you're telling me they have to stand down because numbers are magically appearing on old tombstones. That's a bunch of voodoo crap. We got to get going here. Time is money," bellowed the box store's project chief.

Feeling pressured, Billings decided to go public about the Granby graveyard occurrence to gain more time to probe the phenomenon. But he never expected the brief account he gave to the *Manchester Chronicle* to create a firestorm. Almost immediately the national press jammed the society's phone lines and emails, and when Billings returned to the Granby site with Corey and Fran, they encountered a throng of television news trucks and reporters.

"Show us the invisible numbers," shouted several reporters, and Billings decided to oblige them.

"If this doesn't happen again, we're going to look damn ridiculous," he muttered to his colleagues. "Go ahead Corey. Do a rubbing. The cameras are rolling. This is your Hollywood moment."

Corey gathered his materials and went to the nearest headstone, his every move carefully chronicled by several video cameras.

"You can see there is no date on this monument. I'll now take a rubbing of its surface and you'll see what happens," announced Corey.

"Here goes nothing," whispered a worried Billings to Fran.

As Corey moved his lumberman's chalk against the paper at the bottom of the headstone, the now familiar date reappeared.

"It says *August 11, 2012*," observed a reporter, causing a wave of murmurs among his cohorts.

"Thank God," sighed Billings, patting Fran on the shoulder. "But how the hell is this happening?"

A long round of questions from the assembled reporters followed the demonstration. All three members of the historical society continued to be at a loss to provide a plausible explanation for the appearance of the date on the rubbing.

"Sorry, but we just don't know what's going on here. As you can see, there's no date on the stones, but one appears when a rubbing is done. Perhaps one of you would like to try it?" inquired Billings.

"I'll do it," responded a woman Lionel recognized from a local television station.

"Great! Fran, give her a hand, would you?"

"Sure," she replied, holding a piece of rice paper against a different headstone and instructing the reporter how to move the chalk against it.

"Oh my God, there it is!" exclaimed the newsperson as the cryptic alphanumeric symbols appeared. "Is this some kind of trick paper?"

"No ma'am. It's standard Aqaba gravestone rubbing paper. If you have a regular piece of paper, you can try it," responded Billings.

"I do," said the reporter, tearing a sheet from her notebook.

"Go ahead, Karen...rub it."

"You know my name?" responded the correspondent as she moved the chalk across the paper.

"Watch you on the news," answered Billings.

As soon as the first few letters of the date appeared, the gathering rumbled in astonishment.

"This is...*amazing*. What does it mean? The date must have some significance!" exclaimed the dumbfounded reporter.

"Like I said, we're as much in the dark about it as you are, but we're going to continue our investigation of the site in hopes of coming up with some answers," offered Billings.

✄

That evening the local media, as well as the national networks, carried accounts of the incident unfolding in Granby. By the next day the number of reporters at the cemetery had increased three-fold and police had to cordon off the area. By week's end, media from across the globe had descended on the small community. Droves of curiosity-seekers showed up as well. Inundated by requests for information, the historical society held a news conference, headlined by the state's lieutenant governor, Max Harrington.

"At this point, Mr. Billings and his staff continue to investigate this unusual occurrence. A team of paranormal experts and forensic specialists will join them in an attempt to solve this mystery. Mr. Billings, would you like to add anything?" inquired Harrington.

"*Ah*, not really. I think you've pretty well covered...*things*," replied Billings, stepping away from the microphone.

The lieutenant governor watched Billings as he receded to the background and then he added, "Well, okay. I guess that's it. We'll let you know what's going on as soon as we know, er...what's going on. Thank you."

"What the hell else can I say about this thing? Maybe we need to bring in David Copperfield," mumbled Billings into Corey's ear.

The crowd at the site increased substantially each day as teams of investigators from a host of universities and government agencies attempted to discover the secret of the Granby apparition. As the weeks passed, nothing was resolved, but great speculation as to its meaning flooded the Internet and airwaves. Most were apocalyptic in nature. August 11, 2012 was declared the new *End Time*, and millions of people around the globe were preparing for it.

Meanwhile, national leaders attempted to mitigate the fears of their citizens, but reason was supplanted by growing panic and in many places order began to breakdown. There were skeptics, but the incomprehensible manifestation of the headstone's date was proof enough for most of the planet's inhabitants that Earth's days were numbered. Even *The New York Times* proclaimed, "This one is different," concluding that no prediction of Armageddon was ever preceded by such a mystifying and supernatural communiqué.

In an effort to disburse the vast crowds that had flocked to Granby, state officials decided to remove the headstones from their site. The town had run out of food and other essentials and locals were in a dither. When authorities appeared to dig up the gravestones, they were met with opposition. The multitudes surrounded the half dozen state workers and threatened to harm them if they so much as touched the ground around what it termed the "sacred markers." Fearing for their lives, the would-be gravediggers quickly threw down their shovels and departed.

By the time the sun rose on August 11, 2012, in Granby, the world had experienced a level of lawlessness and chaos never before seen. As the appointed time unfolded, the civil unrest subsided, and as it approached midnight on what most of the world's population believed was doomsday, crowds gathered in city squares and parks and waited for human existence to end. But it did not. The hands of the clock continued to move, and it became

August 12, 2012. Conceiving that it was just another false prophecy, the assembled masses breathed a sigh of relief and returned to the routine of their lives.

✂

Fifty light-years away on Gliese 667, six trillion spectators—watching eight hundred ten-mile long JumboTron screens—roared with pleasure at the finale of "Galaxy Gotcha," a reality show presented by the Office of Giliesian Amusement. In the Imperial Stadium, the viewers chanted "More! More!" with their limbs outstretched toward their monarch. King Groidro Phrobe rose and signaled for silence with his six glimmering appendages.

"You wish more? Then *more* you shall have," proclaimed the king, pointing his royal scepters in the direction of Earth.

At the Granby graveyard, the crowds had departed, leaving only Billings, Corey, and Fran. They had returned in the off chance that something might have changed when they took a *post*-August 11, 2012 rubbing.

"*What the...?*" exclaimed Billings, as his chalk moved across the bottom of a headstone revealing a new inscription—*November 14, 2012.*

On Giliese 667, the cheers of satisfaction were deafening.

190

IVON PREFONTAINE

Summer Ends

He lit down oh so gently
He posed oh so perfectly.
I heard him say;
I really did!
"Take my picture please
My time almost done
This serves as a final memorial."
I took his picture
He stood oh so still
Posed oh so gratefully
Once done, he took his leave, gracefully
Both our jobs nearly done.

ELLARAINE LOCKIE

The Last War

The woman I meet on the street
leaving her SUV wears a sable coat in August
Tomorrow sweat will slide
down her sundress like butter in the sun
The weather as out of balance
as the California budget
She may or may not know the trees
lining the cul-de-sac are dying before their time
Already the acacia has told hummingbirds
it's too tired to serve their fourteen meals every hour

If she had been in Montana last month
she'd have known that the sky cried long and hard
in record breaking depression and the ten year
droughted ground couldn't absorb the tears
That ensuing floods washed
the Rocky Mountain Reservation down
the Bear Paw Mountains into a national disaster

The woman walks toward her Eichler
Ancestor cousin to the ancient houses in Pompeii
with no connection to the street
other than the door through which she disappears
Architecture that turns its back to the world and looks
into an atrium, entire walls of glass and private garden
The kind of isolation that money can buy in a city

So maybe the woman doesn't know Mother Nature
is revolting all over the world
We sink mine shafts into her body
in order to boast shiny baubles on our fingers
We drag out the rest of her entrails
if we haven't already dumped poison down them
Drain her lifeblood for bigger and better
Kill her offspring for sport and strip her naked
Who can blame her if she shakes with anger
Pours her wrath over us
Fights back with any weapon she possesses

➢

Mother Earth will win this war
when she leaves cells of her spawn alive
After the descendants of the woman
whose sprinklers flood the sidewalk
are all swallowed, starved, smashed or buried
by the holocaust of consequences
Any mother would do the same

First published in *Mobius, the Poetry Magazine* (nominated for a 2011 Pushcart Prize)

ELLARAINE LOCKIE

Ripe at Harvest

She's 13 and pure as the Montana air she breathes
He's a bronze and muscled 16
A kid on the road with his Oklahoma uncles
Come to harvest her family's wheat
Asks *Any of y'all wash and iron shirts*
She'll make her mother stay up an extra
two hours to learn

She keeps the pile in her room overnight
Has trouble sleeping and when she does
Dreams of riding on the slow rock
of a black stallion's back
She won't know the word *pheromone*
until she follows her first boyfriend to college

Here and now she knows only that she wants
to deliver all their lunches to the combine crew
They take her to the county fair on Sunday
When even wheat bursting from its beards
has to learn to wait
That night on the Ferris wheel
the Oklahoma Kid takes her hand in his
Starts one of those brushfires that gets
out of control real fast in August

She's ready for this, been practicing
on her pillow since she was 10
and saw Rock Hudson kiss Doris Day
But then Oklahoma asks if he can collect
his shirts in the morning
before they move on to the next farm
Steam rising at midnight

First published in *Ibbetson Street*

BRUCE WEIGL

My Dimension

Beautiful weather here now,
        If you're blind. Summer
                With that fall bite in the night air,
        And through my window,
                The tree frogs' hum like a flood.
                      We don't like redundancies.
We think only other people repeat their stories.
                    I thought I saw a world.
        I thought I saw someone's
Boot on someone else's neck.

From *TriQuarterly*, Winter/Spring 2011

DIANE WAKOSKI

Steelman Tears Up the Summer Garden

The Snowy Owl has her own garden
wherein she transforms summer
atop the tallest sunflower's drooping head,
her white feathers like drifts of crystal travertine.

The Blue Ice Wolf reminds me to stand
as upright as sunflower stalks.

The panther has wrapped its obsidian
shawl-like flowing self around my shoulders—with
this wrap I know it's time
to leave my rooms full
of summer ghosts and friends.

But I am not ready for my journey. In fact,
it is the terror I daily suppress
into my asthma, my arthritic knee,
my degenerating lumbar vertebrae,
the needle in my gold tooth,
the stage pulleys on my chest.

Not ready, not ready, I say
to the Snowy Owl, wintry feathers sloped over the sunflowers,
waiting to fly ahead and make a path.

Not ready, not ready, I say
to the Blue Ice Wolf standing in
my room's corner, waiting for me to climb astride
his ice-chipped back.

Not ready, not ready, I say
to the Black Smoke Panther on my shoulders
who will keep me woven into his shadow
for the journey.

Odd, I've never been one to pack until
the last minute before a trip. Steelman—
he's always ready weeks in advance.
Maybe it's no different this time? Or perhaps
it even makes more sense? What
would I need, or actually what would I be permitted
to take in my old valise?

Snowy Owl,
Blue Ice Wolf,
Smoke Panther
will know
when it's time.
            (So, so not ready, I keep saying.)
Nevertheless, without baggage
we will begin our descent from this dry summer's garden
to Persephone's Underworld
of urchin blue flowers.

DALE SPROWL

The End of Summer

On the doorstep sits the end of summer—
    A beach chair
    Two towels
    An empty propane tank and
    A sprinkler game to attach to the end of a hose.
The Welcome Summer sign will be put away for another year.
The children are back in school.

PART XII
SUN, MOON & STARS

The Sun

you puny star!
there will come
a day when I will
not worship you!

when your light
will merely
grow
grass over my grave!

& then, like me,
you will crumble,
& be scattered into
gigantic red flames

scorching this planet,
making crisp
those who have laid
blankets at your feet,

built temples in your honor,
christened you
with a thousand
different names,

never once
making you feel *this* small
you puny star!
you, sun.

CARL SANDBURG

Back Yard

Shine on, O moon of summer.
Shine to the leaves of grass, catalpa and oak,
All silver under your rain tonight.

An Italian boy is sending songs to you tonight from an accordion.
A Polish boy is out with his best girl; they marry next month;
    tonight they are throwing you kisses.

An old man next door is dreaming over a sheen that sits in a
    cherry tree in his back yard.

The clocks say I must go—I stay here sitting on the back porch drinking
    white thoughts you rain down.

    Shine on, O moon,
Shake out more and more silver changes.

Summer Grass

Summer grass aches and whispers
It wants something; it calls and it sings; it pours
        Out wishes to the overhead stars.
The rain hears; the rain answers; the rain is slow
        Coming; the rain wets the face of the grass.

Summer Stars

Bend low again, night of summer stars.
So near you are, sky of summer stars,
 So near, a long-arm man can pick off stars,
Pick off what he wants in the sky bowl,
So near you are, summer stars,
So near, strumming, strumming,
So lazy and hum-strumming.

DALE SPROWL

Castle by the Sea (Castellammare)

On the cliff above, Joseph Cotten's tennis court jutted;
below the street curved past Lola Lane's Spanish mansion
(the speakeasy where they discovered Thelma Todd's body).
Down a half-mile to Sunset Boulevard we walked past John Barrymore's
villa and bought Health Bars or ice cream drumsticks at the liquor store.

We climbed over the landslide of the house that slid from
the hilltop where the twins from *Babes in Toyland* lived;
like Dorothy's Kansas house, it landed next to the house
where the Bahai family came to live in the Sixties.

Next door a stairway led to the footbridge over the Coast Highway
that took us to the beach where our parents played bridge on Sundays
(they played with magnetic cards so the wind wouldn't blow them away).
Once when they weren't there, we swam alone with seaweed necklaces.

We hunted for moonstones among pebbles washed up by the tides;
creamy and white, they become translucent when polished,
lucent like the phosphorescence we saw in the water at night.
When the grunion ran, the beach filled with tiny slivers
that shimmered and flipped in the moon's light.

We'd trick or treat at Batman's butler's house
and at the castle by the sea above the Getty property.
Chucko the birthday clown wished me a happy day on his show,
and once I appeared in Miss Mary's magic mirror on KTLA.

When we got older, we dressed up like the Beatles and sang
"I Want to Hold Your Hand" on TV, a "gig" the European plate spinners,
the Amazing Carlsons got us. A bit later, our television careers in tact,
we stood behind Peter and Gordon as they performed on the beach at sunset.

My real fairytale childhood lives on.

First published as "Castle by the Sea" in *Moon Over Continent's Edge* (Finishing Line Press, 2009)

JOHN BRANTINGHAM

Afterwards I Stayed Outside for an Hour Before They Made Me Come In

I must have been eleven,
(or maybe I was twelve)
the first time I noticed a satellite.

It was the first really warm day of summer
in 1982 (or maybe it was 1983)
when the wind coming off the desert
had blown the smog out of L.A.
and the street lights
seemed to glare less than
usual, and that satellite crossed Orion,
the one constellation I knew, until it
got lost behind the orange
tree in my parent's backyard.

By the time I'd climbed on
top of the garage to see it
again, it had vanished, and I
stood staring at each star individually—
squinting at each one, comparing
all of them to the stars nearby
making sure they stayed still—to see
if they too would lose their
grip on the night
and fall away into the sky.

JOHN BRANTINGHAM

Sometimes at Night, It Falls on Me Still

In 1979, Skylab lost its grip
on night and fell to Earth,
and no one knew where it would
land, but we were all afraid it might rip
through the sky like a bomb
arcing past the USSR and China
and the Son of Sam,
and that on some late night, it
might burst silently through the clouds
until it found the roof under
which we lay
and that it might crush us
as we slept,
and we would never even know we died.

JOHN BRANTINGHAM

In Praise of Dogs Who Howl at the Moon

Some nights,
everything on Earth is loose,
and you feel yourself slipping off gravity's
mooring, slipping off into
the night, feel the moon's going to grab
you and pull you out into space
and slingshot you past Mars and Jupiter
out to where Pluto
and all the rest of the solar system's losers live,
out where you will never see
you wife laugh the way she
laughs when you do your impression of her father,
laugh the way a person can laugh only
when it's funny but she's ashamed too,
laugh with the wild joy of a bear
waking up after months of sleep—
on those nights you want to grab onto something
wedged deep and tight as a burr in a furry ear
and scream your complaints at the moon
as the dogs howl
and the bears roar and everyone shouts
together—you want to yell that no one
belongs out there in the cold with Pluto
that we belong here where summer love is
and anyone who loves and howls
is one of Earth's favorite children.

JEFFREY ALFIER: As a poet, I take in the world around me, observe potential poem triggers, and make mental or written notes—raw data I work on later to build the poem. In "Late Summer at Café Catalonia," I recorded what I saw and heard while eating in a café in Tucson, Arizona, though I've given it a fictional name. It was frequented by workers, farmers, and their families—a strong local feel. Though seemingly a simple, ordinary setting, it was for me a grand landscape of poetic possibilities. I write poems of place, filled with tactile imagery of settings and characters that populate the verse. The café was perfect for this.

DANIEL PATRICK DELANEY: "Summer Nights and the Short Wave Radio" is about a quest for independence and the yearning to become an adult in order to escape my captivity as an unwanted orphan living with an aunt and uncle, along with their nine children. The short wave radio was my link to the outside world and some sense of belonging. It also introduced me to one of my boyhood heroes, Jean Shepherd—for that alone I am grateful. This is an excerpt from an unfinished manuscript.

KIRSTEN DIERKING ("The Ordinary"): A few summers ago, I challenged myself to write a completely new poem every day for fourteen days. It was summer, and I ended up writing a lot of poems about small things that were going on out in the yard—and one day I wrote about mowing the lawn. I did revise this poem later, but most of it—the pink shorts, the red mower, and dragonfly—were all images from that one particular summer day.

PAUL FERICANO: My father, Frank Paul Fericano, was a WWII navy veteran who survived the near sinking of the USS Franklin during the battle of Okinawa on March 19, 1945. When a single enemy plane dropped two armor-piercing bombs, he and dozens of others became trapped in the dark, below deck in a flooded compartment. He was certain he was going to die that day, but eventually made his way topside. He witnessed hundreds of shipmates killed that morning and for years could never talk about the war. In 2001, I tape-recorded several conversations with my father in which he talked about his life. One of the stories he vividly recalled was the incident I write about in my poem, "The Day I Almost Died." "When I saw your body go limp," he recounted to me, "I immediately thought of all those men on my ship." My father passed away in 2005 at the age of eighty-one.

RODGER JACOBS ("Pynchon at Craigville Beach"): The piece is from a section called "Writers at the Shore," part of a volume of collected short pieces called *Invisible Ink*, which was hailed as "the most exemplary L.A. book of 2012" by *CityWatch L.A.*

JAX NTP: "ante meridiem III" is a sharp desire that lingers beyond winter, lingers beyond the stench of horse piss on murk snow, a desire so vague that it carries over to the summer. "ante meridiem VIII" is about a summer fling, summer lust that is yet to happen, but the speaker indulges within the moment before the physical act. "ante meridiem X" the summer lust of young love, revisited, but the abstract desire has manifested itself, lust materialized into something more, but not yet love, perhaps even more than love.

JASON PARKER ("Soaking Up The Sun"): This excerpt from my upcoming novel *Soul Synthesis* was written immediately after hearing a quote by Pete Postlethwaite sampled in a minimal techno composition by Extrawelt while under the almost summer sun. It went as follows: "We wouldn't be the first life form to wipe itself out. But what would be unique about us is that we did it knowingly. What does that say about us? The question I've been asking is: why didn't we save ourselves when we had the chance? Is the answer because on some level we weren't sure if we were worth saving?"

BART PLANTENGA ("Summer Mid-Manhattan"): Furman Pivo believes he + beer may be the cause of a rash of streetlight outages. This sense of empowerment transforms him into the Beer Mystic. He has a mission and a mandate. Or does he? In any case, New York City will never be the same, and the rest is history or myth or delusion. Interested readers can find more of the story at: http://bartyodel3.wordpress.com/about/

JACKIE PLEDGER-SKWERSKI: It was love at first sight when I first saw the Redwood Community Forest in Arcata, California. My husband, Art, and I had driven there to take my son, Peter, to grad school at Humboldt State University. A creative person, Peter was there to study theatrical lighting, but he loved nature—the ocean, sunrises, sunsets, and now the redwoods. One day, he said that if he ever died, he wanted his ashes sifted in the ocean, where he surfed, and among the redwoods that he loved so much. He died five years ago of a heart attack at thirty-four. We had him cremated and plan to carry out his request in the near future.

JOAN JOBE SMITH ("Endless Summers"): The poem, dedicated to my son, former surfer Danny Bryan Horgan, was first published after winning first prize in *Surfer* magazine's 1997 poetry competition, and next appeared in *Pearl* (2000). In 2009, the poem received a Long Beach (California) Arts Council-City Transit Award and is on permanent display at the Long Beach First Street Transit Gallery. Soon, 48th Street Press will publish the poem as a broadsheet.

LARRY D. THOMAS: Inasmuch as poems are "made things," most of my poetry bubbles up from the springs of my imagination. I enjoy the difficult challenge of making my imaginative poems so faithful to their subject matter, whatever it may be, that they come across to the reader as convincingly "real." Every once in a while, however, I experience things that beg for representation in poems. Such was the case with both "Apricots" and "The Night We Were Gods." For twenty or so years running, my wife and I have made at least one trip annually to the Santa Fe/Taos area of northern New Mexico. We absolutely love the place, its history, multiplicity of cultures, weather, and natural beauty. During one of our pilgrimages, we decided to stroll the streets near the historical plaza area in Santa Fe, and bathe ourselves in the dying light of the day. That is when we rounded a corner and came upon those ripe apricots, scattered all over the side of the street beneath the tree. They glowed in the marvelous evening light as if lit from within. "The Night We Were Gods" came along when we were visiting friends in Houston. They lived in a loft-like apartment that was once a department store. The glass hummingbirds were hanging from the entryway to their kitchen area. Our friends loved candles so the only light in the apartment that evening was candlelight. When the hummingbirds gently moved back and forth in the air currents, they sparkled in the darkness as if aglow, so we were drawn to touch them without realizing it. Later, when we returned to our home and looked in a mirror, we noticed a thin streak of glitter that we had unconsciously spread on our eyelids while rubbing our eyes. It was one of the most magical moments either of us had ever experienced.

THOMAS M. THOMAS ("AM Radio," "Barefoot Days," "Palm Springs"): Summer always makes me think of when I was younger and I didn't have to think of school for a few months. I took my shoes off and only wore them when I had to. Summer was when I suddenly grew up and noticed girls for the first time. And summer was when I could go to the beach or the desert for a couple of weeks and spend hours in the water.

EDDIE WOODS: "The Dawn of Reality" reflects how I eventually felt about my lover at the time having an affair with a friend to whom I'd introduced her. At first I didn't mind, and actually embraced their romance. I was away the entire summer, traveling with the 'tipi people' to the free festivals all over England and Wales. But once back in London, I began seeing things differently. Especially when the lady refused to stop sleeping with my friend, even though I'd asked her to. Thankfully our relationship survived this little bump in the road. While the friend and I remain close to this day. "Retour New York-Amsterdam" was inspired by a book with the same title. Compiled by the Dutch photographer and journalist Sacha de Boer, it contains interviews with sixteen artists, eight of whom are Americans living in Amsterdam and the other eight Dutch artists who reside in New York. Published in 2009, it coincided with the four hundredth anniversary celebrations of Henry Hudson's historic 1609 expeditionary voyage up what is now the Hudson River and the subsequent founding of New Amsterdam (which later became New York, after British forces seized it from the Dutch). Of the sixteen artists in *Retour New York-Amsterdam*, I am the only writer. The rest are painters, photographers, and sculptors. Plus, yes, no more flying in airplanes for this Amsterdam-based New Yorker! The English text of Sacha's interview with me can be read at http://eddiewoods.nl/about/eddie-woods-interview/

JOANIE HIEGER FRITZ ZOSIKE: "'S' Is for Summer" is part of a poem cycle, *An Alphabet of Love*—which does not presume to be "the" alphabet…it is "an" alphabet. There are many possible alphabets. I offer you mine, with love.

ABOUT THE AUTHORS

JEFFREY C. ALFIER is a three-time Pushcart Prize nominee, and a 2010 nominee for the UK's Forward Prize for Poetry. In 2012, he was nominated for a Breadloaf scholarship. In 2006, he received honorable mention for the Rachel Sherwood Poetry Prize, and in 2005 won first place awards from the Redrock Writer's Guild of Utah and the Arizona State Poetry Society. He holds an MA in Humanities from California State University at Dominguez Hills. Having served twenty-seven years in the U.S. Air Force, he is a member of Iraq and Afghanistan Veterans of America (IAVA). He's also worked as a functional analyst with Science Applications International Corporation, and once taught history for City College of Chicago's European Division. His credits include *Birmingham Poetry Review, Connecticut Review, Tulane Review, Pea River Journal, Los Angeles Review, New York Quarterly, Pearl Magazine* and *Poetry Ireland Review*. His chapbooks are *Strangers Within the Gate* (2005), *Offloading the Wounded* (2009), *Before the Troubadour Exits* (2010), *Bluesman's Daughter* (2010), *The Torch Singer* (2011), *The Gathering Light at San Cataldo* (2012), and *The City Without Her* (2012). He serves as co-editor of *San Pedro River Review*.

WILLIAM BLAKE (1757-1827) was an English poet, painter, and printmaker. For the most part unrecognized during his lifetime, Blake is now considered one of the greatest poets of all time in any language. As a visual artist, he has been lauded by one art critic as "far and away the greatest artist Britain has ever produced."

JOHN BRANTINGHAM'S poetry and fiction have been published in hundreds of magazines and venues, including Garrison Keillor's *Writer's Almanac, Pearl, Tears in the Fence, Confrontation*, and *The Journal*. His books include *East of Los Angeles* and *Let Us All Pray to Our Own Strange Gods* (forthcoming from World Parade Books). He works at Mt. San Antonio College, where he teaches English and directs the creative writing programs.

JULIE CADAWALLADER-STAUB lives near Burlington, Vermont. Her poems have been published in numerous journals and featured on Garrison Keillor's *The Writer's Almanac*. Her first collection of poems, *Face to Face*, was published in 2010. *Joy* and *Guinea Pig*, which Garrison Keillor read on *The Writer's Almanac*, are in this collection, in addition to sixty other poems. Julie's poem *Reverence* has been anthologized in Garrison Keillor's book *Good Poems: American Places*.

ANTON CHEKHOV (1860-1904) was a Russian physician, playwright, and author considered to be among the greatest writers of short stories. His classic plays include *The Seagull, Uncle Vanya, Three Sisters*, and *The Cherry Orchard*.

VIRGINIE COLLINE is a French translator living in Paris. Her poems have appeared in *The Scrambler, Notes from the Gean, Prune Juice, Frostwriting, Haiku Journal, Prick of the Spindle, Mouse Tales Press, StepAway Magazine, BRICKrhetoric, Seltzer, Overpass Books, Dagda Publishing, The Four Quarters Magazine* and *Yes, Poetry,* among others.

DANIEL PATRICK DELANEY lives in a suburb of Philadelphia with his wife and three children. He and his wife own a string of coffee shops located in medical centers in the Philadelphia area.

COLLEEN DELEGAN, a writer and producer, lives in Chicago. She spent five years in Europe and Asia, collecting material and traveling extensively. She has written pilots for NBC, CBS, and ABC in addition to several screenplays. In a previous life, Colleen was president of her own advertising agency, "Delegan & Kimmel, Words & Pictures," and was a creative director for Leo Burnett, U.S.A. Her first book, *Three Thousand Coffees in Vienna*, was published in 2004. She is currently under contract to ghostwrite a murder mystery.

KIRSTEN DIERKING's third book of poems, *Tether*, was released by Spout Press in June 2013. She is the author of two previous books of poetry, *Northern Oracle* (Spout Press, 2007) and *One Red Eye* (Holy Cow! Press, 2001). Her poems have been heard on *The Writer's Almanac* and have appeared in numerous journals and anthologies, including Garrison Keillor's *Good Poems, American Places* and *To Sing Along the Way: Minnesota Women Poets from Pre-Territorial Days to the Present*. She is the recipient of a 2010 McKnight Artist Fellowship, a Minnesota State Arts Board Grant for literature, a Loft Literary Center Career Initiative Grant, a SASE/Jerome Grant, and a writing residency at the Banfill-Locke Center for the Arts. She teaches humanities courses at Anoka-Ramsey Community College.

DAVID DONDERO is a musician who is perpetually on tour. NPR's *All Songs Considered* named David one of the "best living songwriters." His tenth album is a sixteen-song retrospective titled *Golden Hits Vol. 1*. This album was released on Unrequited Records, which will also put out his next album *This Guitar*, due in stores Fall 2013.

PAUL LAURENCE DUNBAR (1872-1906)—a poet, novelist, and playwright—was the first African American writer to gain national prominence. Born in Dayton, Ohio, he was the son of ex-slaves. Dunbar lived only to age thirty-three, but in his short life created a large body of work—writing short stories, novels, librettos, plays, songs, essays, and poetry.

BARBARA EKNOIAN's work has appeared in *PEARL, Chiron Review, Re)verb,* and *Cradle Song*, a motherhood anthology. She has received two Pushcart Prize nominations, and is a member of Donna Hilbert's poetry workshop in Long Beach, California. Her fiction was featured in the 2009 Sixth Annual Emerging Voices Show produced by Sally Shore's New Short Fiction Series. She hails from New Jersey and has never lost her accent.

MERRILL FARNSWORTH is a Nashville-based writer, artist, and therapist. Born among the Texas tumbleweeds, Merrill came of age reveling in the sights and sounds of Puerto Rico's Afro-Caribbean culture. The cadences of South Carolina left their mark on her, as did melodies reaching from Appalachia to the Mississippi Delta. She is a published poet and award-winning lyricist, and recently collaborated with Phil Madeira on the Americana release *Mercyland*. In 2012, Silver Birch Press published *Jezebel's Got the Blues...And Other Works of Imagination*, Merrill's collection of performance pieces that was selected for 2012's The Puzzle, a festival of plays held in New York City. For more about Merrill, visit www.writingcircle.org.

PAUL FERICANO is a poet and satirist and co-founder (with Elio Ligi) of the first parody news syndicate, *Yossarian Universal News Service* (1980). His work has appeared in *The Wormwood Review, The New York Quarterly* and *Projector,* and his books of poetry include: *Commercial Break; Sinatra, Sinatra;* and *Loading the Revolver with Real Bullets*. In the forthcoming year *The New Yorker, The Atlantic Monthly,* and *The Paris Review* are all expected to reject his work. Visit Paul at www.yunews.com.

CHRIS FORHAN, born and raised in Seattle, Washington, is the author of three books of poetry: *Black Leapt In*, winner of the Barrow Street Press Poetry Prize; *The Actual Moon, The Actual Stars*, winner of the Morse Poetry Prize and a Washington State Book Award; and *Forgive Us Our Happiness*, winner of the Bakeless Prize. He is also the author of two chapbooks, *x* and *Crumbs of Bread*, and his poems have appeared in *Poetry, Paris Review, Ploughshares, New England Review, Parnassus*, and other magazines, as well as in *The Best American Poetry*. He has won a National Endowment for the Arts Fellowship and two Pushcart Prizes and has been a resident at Yaddo and a fellow at Bread Loaf. Silver Birch Press will publish his chapbook *Ransack and Dance* in July 2013. He lives with his wife, the poet Alessandra Lynch, and their two sons, Milo and Oliver, in Indianapolis, where he teaches at Butler University.

SUSIE SWEETLAND GARAY: Born and raised in Portland Oregon, Susie received a Bachelor's degree in English Literature from Brigham Young University, spent some years in the Ohio Appalachians, and currently lives in the Willamette Valley with her husband and cat where she works in the vineyard industry. She spends her free time writing, growing plants, and making art. She has been published in a variety of journals, on line and in print, and co-edits *The Blue Hour* literary magazine, thebluehourmagazine.com.

JEFFREY GRAESSLEY lives in La Puente, California. His poems can be found in the upcoming volumes of *Emerge Literary Journal* and *RCC MUSE Magazine*. His first chapbook, *Her Blue Dress* will be published in the Silver Birch Press *Pieces of Silver Anthology* (Fall 2013). His recent discovery of the Beat generation has prompted loving and longing thoughts for that simple, drunken, far-gone time in American history.

SYED AFZAL HAIDER is a writer and founding editor of *Chicago Quarterly Review*. His short stories and essays have appeared in a variety of literary magazines including *Saint Ann's Review, AmerAsia, Rambunctious Review, The Journal of Pakistani Literature, The Taylor Trust, Trajectory, Marco Polo*. Indian Voices, Oxford University Press, Milkweed Editions, Penguin Books, and Longman Literature have anthologized Haider. His short story collection, *Tumbleweed Connection,* was a finalist for the 2004 MVP competition. His first novel, *To Be With Her,* was published in 2010, and his second novel, *Life of Ganesh*, is forthcoming. He lives in Evanston, Illinois, with his wife and is father of two wonderful grown-up sons. He can be reached by email at sahaider@sbcglobal.net.

WIN HARMS is a poet living in France with her professor husband. She hails from the state of the cowboy poetry contest, but she has lived pretty much everywhere, including many psych wards, and considers herself a survivor of the struggle. The chaos has ceased and now she spends her time doing needlepoint and laundry, but longs to share her words with the world. As of last year, she left her roaring twenties, and is now feeling fecund and free.

DONNA HILBERT's latest book, *The Green Season,* World Parade Books, a collection of poems, stories, and essays, is now available in an expanded second edition. Donna appears in and her poetry is the text of the documentary *Grief Becomes Me: A Love Story*, a Christine Fugate film. Earlier books include *Mansions* and *Deep Red* from Event Horizon, *Transforming Matter* and *Traveler in Paradise* from Pearl Editions, and the short story collection *Women Who Make Money and the Men Who Love Them* from Staple First Editions (published in England). Poems in Italian can be found in Bloc notes 59 and in French in *La page blanche*, in both cases translated by Mariacristina Natalia Bertoli. New work is in recent or forthcoming issues of *5AM, Nerve Cowboy, Pearl,* and *Poets & Artists*. A new collection, *The Congress of Luminous Bodies,* is forthcoming from Aortic Books. Learn more at www.donnahilbert.com.

RODGER JACOBS has won multiple awards and grants for his work as a journalist, documentary writer and producer, screenwriter, playwright, magazine editor, true crime writer, book critic and columnist for *PopMatters*, and live event producer. In 2010, he provided the preface and original inspiration for *Jack London: San Francisco Stories* (Sydney Samizdat Press). He is the author of the novel *The Furthest Palm,* published by Silver Birch Press in 2012.

DIANE EAGLE KATAOKA lives at eight thousand feet in the Eastern Sierra, where she skis and hikes. A researcher for the late Leon Uris *(Trinity* and *The Haj),* she was director of marketing and communications for the Music Academy of the West, as well as editor-in-chief of the *Mammoth Times* and *Mammoth Sierra Magazine*. She is currently a freelance writer and editor, poet, and blogger. (Visit her blog at mammothlakesview.com.) Her chapbook *Snow Globe,* published by Two Birds Press, is a poetic history of five seasons in a mountain ski town.

MICHAEL C. KEITH is the author of over twenty books on electronic media, among them *Talking Radio, Voices in the Purple Haze, Radio Cultures, Signals in the Air*, and the classic textbook *The Radio Station*. The recipient of numerous awards in his academic field, he is also the author of dozens of journal articles and short stories and has served in a variety of editorial positions. In addition, he is the author of an acclaimed memoir, *The Next Better Place,* a young adult novel, *Life is Falling Sideways*, and five story anthologies—*Of Night and Light, And Through the Trembling Air, Sad Boy, Hoag's Object,* and *Everything Is Epic* (Silver Birch Press, 2013). He has been nominated for a Pushcart Prize and Pen/O.Henry Award and was a finalist for the National Indie Excellence Award for short fiction anthology.

RUTH MOON KEMPHER, an ex-navy brat who was born in Red Bank, New Jersey, has had her poetry and short prose appear in journals and other periodical publications since 1958, and has published many other people's work since 1994 through her Kings Estate Press in St. Augustine, Florida. She is retired from owning a tavern and from teaching— first for Flagler College while attaining her BA and graduating with the college's first class; and later, after achieving her MA at Emory University in Atlanta, in the English Department of St. Johns River Community College. The latest of her thirty-three (mostly small) collections of verse will also include prose pieces—*Key West Papers* was published by Casa de Cinco Hermanos Press, Pueblo, Colorado. After years of living at the beach, she now lives in the woods in an old cracker house with two dogs, Sadie, a long-legged hound, and Mister Frost, an emotional American Husky.

LINDA KING is a poet, playwright, and artist working in painting and sculpture who was immortalized in the poetry and prose of her former love Charles Bukowski. During the 1970s, King edited the little magazine *Purr*. She also has had her poetry published in a wide variety of magazines, including *The Bukowski Review* and *Wormwood Review*. Her most recent works are the memoir *Loving and Hating Bukowski* and the novel *Mad Ouija*.

TED KOOSER was the United States Poet Laureate from 2004 to 2006 and won a Pulitzer Prize for his book of poems *Delights and Shadows*. He is the author of twelve full-length volumes of poetry and several books of nonfiction, and his work has appeared in many periodicals. He lives in Garland, Nebraska.

THOMAS KUDLA is a graduate of Indiana University, Bloomington. With the help of his tailored degree from the Individualized Major Program at IUB and a grant from the Indiana University Hutton Honors College, he was able to write his first novel, *Confessions of an American*. His book *What My Brain Told Me* was selected as a finalist in the short story nonfiction category of the 2009 National Indie Excellence Awards. For two years, Thom was an editor with the Sun-Times News Group. In 2011, he founded To a T Editorial Group, a manuscript editing business. To learn more about Thom, visit thomkudla.com.

MORIAH LACHAPELL earned her bachelor's degree from Western Oregon University, studied Viticulture at Washington State University, and currently works in horticulture. An Oregon native and resident, she lives in a little town with her daughter and husband. Moriah has been published online and in print and is the editor of the online magazine *The Blue Hour* (thebluehourmagazone.com). You can visit her blog at moriahlachapell.wordpress.com.

ELLARAINE LOCKIE is a widely published and awarded poet, nonfiction book author, and essayist. Her ninth chapbook, *Wild as in Familiar,* was a finalist in the Finishing Line Press Chapbook contest and received *The Aurorean's* Chapbook Pick for Spring 2012. Ellaraine teaches poetry workshops and serves as poetry editor for the lifestyles magazine, *Lilipoh,* and as associate editor for *Mobius*. Silver Birch Press published her chapbook *Coffee House Confessions* in 2013.

GERALD LOCKLIN is a professor emeritus of English at California State University, Long Beach, where he taught full-time from 1965-2007, retains his office and contact information, and still teaches an occasional class as needed. He has published fiction, poetry, essays, and reviews prolifically in periodicals and in over a hundred and fifty books, chapbooks, and broadsides. Recent or upcoming books include a fiction e-Book, *The Sun Also Rises in the Desert,* from Mendicant Bookworks; a collection of poems, *Deep Meanings: Selected Poems, 2008-2013,* from PRESA Press; three simultaneously released novellas from Spout Press; and a French collection of his prose, *Candy Bars: Le Dernier des Damnes* from 13e Note Press, Paris. Event Horizon Press released new editions of *A Simpler Time, A Simpler Place* and *Hemingway Colloquium: The Poet Goes to Cuba* in 2011; Coagula Press released the first of two volumes of his *Complete Coagula Poems;* and *From a Male Perspective* appeared from PRESA Press. In February 2013, Silver Birch Press published *Gerald Locklin: New and Selected Poems (1967-2007),* originally published by World Parade Books (2008). Reach him at gerlocklin@gmail.com, www.geraldlocklin.org, or www.facebook.com/geraldlocklin.

TAMARA MADISON teaches English and French at a public high school in Los Angeles. Raised on a citrus farm in the California desert, Tamara's life has taken her many places, including Europe and the former Soviet Union, where she spent fifteen months in the 1970s. A swimmer and dog lover, Tamara says, "All I ever wanted to do with my life was write, and I mostly write poetry because it suits my lifestyle; I like the way one can say so much in the economical space of a poem."

KAREN MARGOLIS was born in Harare, Zimbabwe, and educated in South Africa and London. She graduated as a mathematician in 1974 and has since moved mainly in the world of words as a freelance author, poet, journalist, editor, broadcaster, and translator. She has lived in Berlin since 1983. Her books include *To Eat or Not to Eat* (1988), and *The Floating Castle* (Kindle 2012), and she has published poems and essays in numerous anthologies and magazines.

CLINT MARGRAVE lives in Long Beach, California. His first full-length collection of poems, *The Early Death of Men,* is newly released from NYQ Books. His work has also appeared or is forthcoming in *The New York Quarterly, Rattle, Ambit* (UK), *3AM* (UK), *Pearl, Serving House Journal, Word Riot,* and *Nerve Cowboy,* among others.

CATFISH MCDARIS'S most infamous chapbook is *Prying with Jack Micheline and Charles Bukowski.* His best readings were in Paris at the Shakespeare and Co. bookstore and with Jimmy "the ghost of Hendrix" Spencer in NYC on 42nd St. He's done over twenty chaps in the last twenty years. He's been in the *New York Quarterly, Slipstream, Pearl, Main St. Rag, Café Review, Chiron Review, Zen Tattoo, Wormwood Review, Great Weather For Media,* and *Graffiti* and been nominated for fifteen Pushcarts, Best of Net. He won the Uprising Award in 1999, and won the Flash Fiction Contest judged by the U.S. Poet Laureate in 2009. He loves cats better than dogs, he misses the New Mexican Mountains, but loves the green of Wisconsin. He retired after thirty-four years at the Main Milwaukee Post Office. He's married to a beautiful Mexican lady and they have a daughter with a tree climbing dog.

DANIEL MCGINN'S work has appeared in the *OC Weekly, Next Magazine,* and other publications. His full-length collection of poems, *1000 Black Umbrellas,* is available from Write Bloody Press. He is currently a student in the low-residency MFA program at Vermont College of Fine Arts. He and his wife are natives of Southern California. They have three children, five grandchildren, and a very good dog.

LORI MCGINN is a mom, grandma, baker of cookies, visual artist, and writer of poems. A native of Whittier, California, her work has appeared in several anthologies and her chapbook, *Waiting*, was published as a part of the Laguna Poets Series.

MARCIA MEARA is a native Floridian living in the Orlando area with her husband of twenty-six years, two silly little dachshunds, and four big, lazy cats. She's fond of reading, gardening, hiking, canoeing, painting, and writing, not necessarily in that order. But her favorite thing in the world is spending time with her seven-year-old granddaughter, the world's funniest little girl. A second grandchild arrived in April 2013. Marcia is currently working on her first book, a romantic thriller set in the Blue Ridge Mountains, which she hopes will prove that it's never too late to follow your dream.

EDNA ST. VINCENT MILLAY (1892-1950) was an American poet and playwright. She received the Pulitzer Prize for Poetry in 1923 for *The Harp Weaver and Other Poems*.

CAROLYN MILLER is a poet and painter living in San Francisco. *Light, Moving,* her most recent book of poetry, was published by Sixteen Rivers Press in 2009, and her first full-length collection, *After Cocteau*, was published by the same press in 2002. Her work has appeared in *The Georgia Review, The Southern Review,* and *The Gettysburg Review,* among other journals, and her awards include the James Boatwright III Prize for Poetry from *Shenandoah*, and the Rainmaker Award from *Zone 3*.

PAUL NEBENZAHL is a writer, musician, and painter living in Evanston, Illinois, and in Sleepy Hollow, New York. As a performing multi-instrumentalist and composer, Paul has created works for film and television, and has performed extensively in theater, stage, and club settings, most recently as Karen Finley's musical director. Paul's poem "*Gusen Station*" was published in English, Italian, and German in 2012 by the *International Committee for Mauthausen and Gusen*. His poem "*Charles Bukowski*" will appear in the Silver Birch Press *Bukowski Anthology* (August 2013). His poetry collection *Black Shroud with Rainbow Fringes* will be published by Silver Birch Press during July 2013.

GERALD NICOSIA, born and raised in Chicago and transplanted to the San Francisco Bay Area in his late twenties, is a poet, fiction writer, biographer, historian, and playwright. He is best known for his biography of Jack Kerouac, *Memory Babe*. Long associated with the Beat and post-Beat writers, he has organized and taken part in hundreds of poetry readings, including a recent Beat reading at Bob Weir's Sweetwater Music Hall in Mill Valley, California, that drew over three hundred people and celebrated the release of the movie version of *On the Road*, on which Nicosia worked as a consultant. He has also spent a good part of his life studying, helping, and chronicling the story of Vietnam veterans; his book *Home to W*ar on their struggle to heal and readjust was picked as one of the "Best Books of 2001" by the *Los Angeles Times*. He is currently at work on a biography of Ntozake Shange, and will publish his fourth book of poetry, *Night Train to Shanghai*, with Creative Arts Books in the summer of 2013. He has also taught and lectured extensively, on the Beats, the Sixties, and modern literature.

JAX NTP is a graduate student at Cal State Long Beach in the Masters of Fine Arts, Creative Writing Program. Her poetry has been featured on KBeach Radio, *Moon Tide Press*, *Subliminal Interiors*, and *The Más Tequila Review*. She is editor-in-chief of CSULB's Literary Journal, *RipRap* Volume 35. "Medusa Sonata" won The Aquarium of the Pacific's 3rd Annual Urban Ocean Poetry Festival in May 2012.

JASON PARKER is the pseudonym of a Californian poet, author, artist, musician, and researcher. He lives on a farm and spends his free time reading and writing about whatever he is passionate about at the time.

BART PLANTENGA is the author of *Beer Mystic*, a novel that circumnavigates the globe in a unique pub crawl. He is also the author of *Wiggling Wishbone*, *Spermatagonia: The Isle of Man*, *Paris Scratch*, and *NY Sin Phoney in Face Flat Minor*. His books include *Yodel-Ay-Ee-Oooo: The Secret History of Yodeling Around the World* and *Yodel in HiFi*. He has been the DJ of *Wreck This Mess* in NYC, Paris and now Amsterdam since 1986. He was a founding member of the NYC-based literary alliance, the Unbearables. He lives and hopes in Amsterdam with his partner Nina and daughter Paloma Jet.

JACKIE PLEDGER-SKWERSKI, following a fifty-year career in business and newspaper journalism, has turned to her true love, fiction. Her feature stories have been published in newspapers and her short stories have appeared in anthologies. She holds a bachelor's degree in education from Purdue University and a master's degree in journalism from Indiana University. She also has taught journalism at Triton Community College (River Grove, Illinois) and Wilbur Wright College (Chicago, Illinois).

STANLEY PLUMLY was born in Barnesville, Ohio, in 1939, and grew up in the lumber and farming regions of Virginia and Ohio. His work has been honored with the Delmore Schwartz Memorial Award and nominations for the National Book Critics Circle Award, the William Carlos Williams Award, and the Academy of Amerian Poets' Lenore Marshall Poetry Prize. He is currently a Distinguished University Professor and Professor of English at the University of Maryland.

IVON PREFONTAINE is a junior high teacher in a small satellite community of Edmonton, Alberta, Canada. He regained an appreciation for poetry and found his way back to it after many years. Poetry has reemerged as an integral aspect of his personal expression and complements a growing meditative practice.

CONRAD ROMO grew up on the other side of the tracks in L.A., short, stocky, and swarthy. He is the producer and host of one of the very best literary reading events in L.A.—Tongue & Groove at the Hotel Café, now in its ninth year. Each month, he blends a handpicked mix of writers to present short fiction, poetry, personal essays, along with a musical guest. His writing has appeared in *Los Angeles Review, Wednesday Magazine, Noveltown, Tu Ciudad, Brooklyn & Boyle, Palehouse, Huizache,* and *Latinos in Lotusland*, and frequently writes for splicetoday.com. Please visit Conrad at the Tongue & Groove website: tongueandgroovela.com.

DANIEL ROMO is the author of the poetry collections *When Kerosene's Involved* (Black Coffee Press, 2013) and *Romancing Gravity* (Silver Birch Press, 2013). His poetry and photography can be found in the *Los Angeles Review, Gargoyle, MiPOesias, Yemassee, Hobart,* and elsewhere. He holds an MFA from Queens University of Charlotte and teaches creative writing. He lives in Long Beach, California. More of his writing can be found at danielromo.net.

CARL SANDBURG (1878-1967) was an American writer and editor, best known for his poetry. He received three Pulitzer Prizes, two for poetry and one for his biography of Abraham Lincoln.

WILLIAM SHAKESPEARE (1564–1616) was a British poet and playwright regarded as the greatest writer in the English language. His works include about forty plays and over one hundred and fifty sonnets.

RAYMOND KING SHURTZ has written over thirty plays, three published with Samuel French and Anchorage Press/Dramatic Publishing. The Founding Artistic Director of Playwright's Workshop Theatre in Phoenix, Arizona, Raymond produced eighty new plays in his twelve-year tenure with the company. In 1998, he began teaching theatre, film, and humanities at Metro Arts, a high school for the performing and visual arts in Phoenix, Arizona, where he taught and produced another ten years of new theatre. His play, *Blue Baby, A Memoir* won the Playwriting Fellowship in 2003 from the Arizona Commission on the Arts. Since 2008, he has worked as a freelance director, actor, writer, and musician. In 2009, Raymond produced and performed his one man show, *Bohemian Cowboy* at The Elephant Theatre, which was the "pick of the week" in *The LA Weekly*, and subsequently performed it approximately seventy-five times in Los Angeles, San Francisco, Southern Utah, and twenty-three shows in Austin, Texas. He also fronts a country/rock/western band, Out on Bail, and performs solo acoustic shows.

TERE SIEVERS lives and works in Long Beach, California. Born and raised on the Jersey shore, she finds inspiration in that East Coast past and this West Coast present. Her poems have appeared in *Pearl, Verve, Black Buzzard Review,* and the Silver Birch Press *Green Anthology* as well as "Your Daily Poem" online.

JOAN JOBE SMITH, founding editor of *Pearl* and *Bukowski Review,* worked for seven years as a go-go dancer before receiving her BA from CSULB and MFA from University of California, Irvine. A Pushcart Honoree, her award-winning work has appeared internationally in more than five hundred publications, including *Outlaw Bible, Ambit, Beat Scene, Wormwood Review,* and *Nerve Cowboy*—and she has published twenty collections, including *Jehovah Jukebox* (Event Horizon Press, US) and *The Pow Wow Cafe* (The Poetry Business, UK), a finalist for the UK 1999 Forward Prize. In July 2012, with her husband, poet Fred Voss, she did her sixth reading tour of England (debuting at the 1991 Aldeburgh Poetry Festival), featured at the Humber Mouth Literature Festival in Hull. In November 2012, Silver Birch Press published her literary profile entitled *Charles Bukowski Epic Glottis: His Art & His Women (& me).* In 2013, World Parade Books will release her memoir *Tales of an Ancient Go-Go Girl.* Her literary magazine *Pearl* will release its fiftieth edition in 2013—find out more at pearlmag.com.

RICK SMITH is a clinical psychologist specializing in brain damage and domestic violence. He writes and plays harmonica for The Mescal Sheiks. His poems have appeared in *South Bay Magazine, Arts and Letters*, *Rattle*, *OnTheBus,* and *Water-Stone*. His most recent books are *The Wren Notebook* (2000), *Hard Landing* (2010), and, forthcoming, *Whispering in a Mad Dog's Ear*, all from Lummox Press.

CLIFTON SNIDER, faculty emeritus at Cal State University, Long Beach, is the internationally acclaimed author of ten books of poetry. A career retrospective of his work, *Moonman: New and Selected Poems*, was published by World Parade Books (2012). His novel about the rise, fall, and physical and spiritual recovery and comeback of a 1980s bisexual rock star, *Loud Whisper* (2000), has been optioned by Iconoclastic Features. His coming out/coming-of-age novel, *Bare Roots,* was published in 2001, as was his novel about two gay Pentecostal preacher's sons, *Wrestling with Angels: A Tale of Two Brothers*. A Jungian/Queer literary critic, his book, *The Stuff That Dreams Are Made On,* was published in 1991, and he has published hundreds of poems, fiction, reviews, and articles internationally. His work has been translated into French. Spanish, and Russian.

DALE SPROWL teaches writing at Biola University in La Mirada, California. During summers, she administrates and teaches at the Young Writer's Project at UCI. Her work with the UCI Writing Project began in 1981, and she has contributed to the UCIWP texts on the teaching of writing. Her first chapbook of poems, *The Colors of Water,* published by Finishing Line Press in 2007, and her second chapbook, *Moon Over Continent's Edge (*2009), have been nominated for a California Book Award. Her poems have also appeared in *Pearl, Fire, A New Song, Ancient Paths,* and *Knowing Stones: Poems of Exotic Places.* She earned her bachelor's degree in humanities and in history as well as a master's degree in history from Pepperdine University. An Educator Associate for the American Psychoanalytic Association, she lives in Newport Beach, California, with her husband.

KENDALL STEINLE grew up in Akron, Ohio. She attended Saint Xavier University in Chicago, along with a stint at the University of Glasgow, receiving her bachelor's in English with minors in Writing and Middle Eastern Studies. Her first publication was in *Journal of Microliterature,* and her stories have appeared in the Silver Birch Press *Silver Anthology* (November 2012) and the Silver Birch Press *Green Anthology* (March 2013). She is currently pursuing her master's degree in Writing and Publishing at DePaul University.

CAITLIN STERN grew up in San Antonio, Texas, where she read in trees, avoided team sports, and 'published' her first book in elementary school. As she grew, she wrote and read more, developing into an avid bibliophile and writer. She followed her love of books to Angelo State University, where she worked as a tutor at her school's Writing Center, and later as a Teaching Assistant while she earned an English MA.

ROBERT LOUIS STEVENSON (1850-1894) was a Scottish novelist, poet, essayist, and travel writer. His most famous works are *Treasure Island, Kidnapped*, and *Strange Case of Dr. Jekyll and Mr. Hyde.* A literary celebrity during his lifetime, Stevenson remains one of the most translated authors in the world.

TATE SWINDELL is a poet, painter, photographer, and filmmaker. His record label, Unrequited Records, has released readings from Herbert Huncke, Harold Norse, and Jack Micheline. Tate and Todd Swindell are currently editing their film about Harold Norse, pulling from their numerous hours of footage shot at the poet's historic Mission flat in San Francisco. He is currently making a film with the poet Neeli Cherkovski.

LARRY D. THOMAS, a member of the Texas Institute of Letters, was privileged to serve as the 2008 Texas Poet Laureate. He has published twenty collections of poems, the most recent of which is *Uncle Ernest* (Virtual Artists Collective, Chicago, 2013). His *Larry D. Thomas: New and Selected Poems* (TCU Press, 2008) was long-listed for the National Book Award.

THOMAS R. THOMAS was born in Los Angeles and grew up in the San Gabriel Valley west of LA. Currently, he lives in Long Beach, California. For his day job, he is a software QA Analyst. He volunteers for Tebot Bach, a community poetry organization, in Huntington Beach. Thomas has been published in *Don't Blame the Ugly Mug: 10 Years of 2 Idiots Peddling Poetry, Creepy Gnome, Carnival, Pipe Dream, Bank Heavy Press, Conceit Magazine, Electric Windmill & Marco Polo.* In November 2012, Carnival released his eChapbook, *Scorpio,* and Washing Machine Press released a chapbooklette called *Tanka.* In 2013, World Parade Books will publish a book of his poetry. Visit his website at thomasrthomas.org.

JERI THOMPSON, a former creative writing major who studied with Elliott Fried and Gerald Locklin at California State University, Long Beach, is currently a blogger (at Trikker Chicks...For Women Who Carve) and regular contributor to *TrikkeWorld* magazine. She can often be found walking around downtown Long Beach in bright blue Pumas or riding on a Trikke (with two Ks). Her poetry has appeared in the Silver Birch Press *Silver Anthology* and the Silver Birch Press *Green Anthology*.

MARY UMANS is a filmmaker and writer living in New York City. Her short film, *The Braddock Boys*, was featured in the 2012 Manhattan Film Festival.

DIRK VELVET is a Poet/Writer of Songs from Muskego, Wisconsin. His writing has been featured in *Beggars and Cheeseburgers, Pearl, Re)verb, Nerve Cowboy,* and *Milwaukee Renaissance*.

PHILIP VERMAAS was born to an actor and stage manager who were touring a play through the otherwise artistically barren towns of the Orange Free State in early 1970s South Africa. For the first months of his life, he lived in a cardboard box among misfit actors and similarly afflicted crew. They called him King Fred. He later despised school and, when finished, refused to participate in any formal tertiary education. Instead he sought education through trial and error and error. He has traveled a bit and spent years in Scotland and a couple in England. Now, through twists of fate, he's holed up in a cottage in semi-rural Johannesburg with his true love while he thinks, writes, smokes, and holds her close. Recently, The Blue Hour published a full length book of his poetry, *Better Cigarettes and Other Poems*.

MELANIE VILLINES is a novelist, playwright, screenwriter, television writer, biographer, editor, and ghostwriter. Her published work includes the novel *Tales of the Sacred Heart* (Bogfire Press), the family memoir *Reason to Fight* (co-written with Hiram Johnson), a celebrity biography *Beyond Hollywood* (co-written with J. Herbert Klein), *Anna & Otto*, a novel for children (Inklings Press), and a variety of ghostwritten books and screenplays. A founding member of Chicago Dramatists, she is the author of twenty plays. Her original screenplays include *Calling Oz*, finalist in the Austin Film Festival and many other screenwriting competitions, and *Just Say the Word*, top-10 finalist in Illinois-Chicago screenwriting competition. She co-wrote the critically acclaimed 90-minute drama *Crime of Innocence*, based on the life of Emmett Till, for the NBC affiliate in Chicago. Her play *Bernice* (co-written with Hiram Johnson) had a February 2013 workshop production in Dallas and her story "Windy City Sinners," an excerpt from her upcoming novel of the same name, will appear in the *Chicago Quarterly Review* (Fall, 2013).

DIANE WAKOSKI has published more than forty collections of poems, including the four books that constitute her series "The Archaeology of Movies and Books"—*Argonaut Rose* (1998), *The Emerald City of Las Vegas* (1995), *Jason the Sailor* (1993), and *Medea the Sorceress* (1991)—all published by Black Sparrow Press; *Emerald Ice: Selected Poems 1962-1987* (1988), which won the Poetry Society of America's William Carlos Williams Award; and *The Collected Greed, Parts 1-13* (1984). She has also published four books of essays: *Toward a New Poetry* (1979), *Variations on a Theme* (1976), *Creating a Personal Mythology* (1975), and *Form Is an Extension of Content* (1972). Her honors include a Fulbright fellowship, a Michigan Arts Foundation award, and grants from the Guggenheim Foundation, the Michigan Arts Council, the National Endowment for the Arts, and the New York State Council on the Arts. She lives in East Lansing, Michigan.

BRUCE WEIGL entered the Army at eighteen and served in Vietnam for one year, beginning in December 1967. He was awarded the Bronze Star and returned to his hometown of Lorain, Ohio, where he enrolled in Lorain County Community College. He earned his BA at Oberlin College, his MA at the University of New Hampshire, and his PhD at the University of Utah. Weigl is the author of more than a dozen books of poetry, including *The Unraveling Strangeness* (2002), *Archeology of the Circle: New and Selected Poems* (1999), and *After the Others* (1999). He has also written several collections of critical essays, has published translations of Vietnamese and Romanian poetry, and has also edited or co-edited several anthologies of war poetry, including *Writing Between the Lines: An Anthology on War and Its Social Consequences* (1997) and *Mountain River: Vietnamese Poetry from the Wars, 1948–1993; A Bilingual Collection* (1998). Weigl's poetry has been widely anthologized, including in *Best American Poetry* (1994), *The Morrow Anthology of Younger American Poets* (1985), *Against Forgetting: Twentieth Century Poetry of Witness* (1993), and *American Alphabets: 25 Contemporary Poets* (2006). Weigl has won the Robert Creeley Award, the Lannan Literary Award for Poetry, the Paterson Poetry Prize, the Poet's Prize from the Academy of American Poets, the Cleveland Arts Prize, and two Pushcart Prizes. *Song of Napalm* (1998) was nominated for the Pulitzer Prize. He has also been awarded fellowships from the National Endowment for the Arts and the Yaddo Foundation.

EDITH WHARTON (1862-1937) was an American novelist and short story writer, and recipient of the 1921 Pulitzer Prize for her novel *The Age of Innocence* (the first woman to receive award), best known for her 1911 novel *Ethan Frome.*

HEATHCOTE WILLIAMS is a poet, playwright, author, and actor. His first book, *The Speakers,* was published in 1964, and he went on to write his epic poems *Whale Nation, Autogedden, Sacred Elephant*, and *Falling for a Dolphin.* Heathcote is also an award-winning playwright. His first full-length play, *AC/DC,* won the Evening Standard Award for Most Promising Play, the George Devine Award and the John Whiting Award. *AC/DC* was chosen as part of the Royal Court's 50th anniversary celebration in 2006. His later play, *The Local Stigmatic,* first played at the Royal Court in 1966 and has since been made into a film by Al Pacino. *The Immortalist* was produced by the National Theatre in London and New York. Heathcote has written and advised on a number of feature films including *Looking for Richard, Hotel,* and *Malatesta.* He has also written extensively for radio and television, including *Hancock's Last Half Hour* and *What the Dickens?* In 2011, Roy Hutchins launched a show of Heathcote's newer poems entitled *Zanzibar Cats* which has had a UK Tour and a run in Edinburgh, where is won the prestigious Herald Archangel Award.

EDDIE WOODS, born 1940 in New York City, is a native alien as opposed to an expatriate. Although an American writer ("The language is far too rich to ever let go of it," he says), Eddie definitely does not see America as 'back home.' For him home is wherever he happens to be. Which, after having traveled and lived in many parts of the world both East and West, since 1978 has mainly been Amsterdam, the Netherlands. It was then that he and Jane Harvey launched *Ins & Outs* magazine and later founded Ins & Outs Press. Always with numerous irons in the literary fire, Eddie regularly appears in various online and print publications. The most recent of his books and spoken-word CDs is *Tsunami of Love: A Poems Cycle.* His website is http://eddiewoods.nl

JOANIE HIEGER FRITZ ZOSIKE is a writer, actor, singer, director, and creative facilitator. Her work has appeared in zines, including *Chez Chez, Helicon Nine, Heresies, International Worker, Jewish Daily Forward, La Mia Ink, Maintenant, Ovation, Womannews* and *Zeitriss*, and is an invited guest blogger on http://www.crocknbunk.com and http://clockwisewise.wordpress.com/2012/12/29/dont-go-changin-by-joanie-fritz-zosike/ (sample post). A veteran of The Living Theatre, she directs the dada/surrealist company, DADAnewyork and is co-founder and co-director of *Action Racket Theatre*. She has just completed a poetry cycle, *An Alphabet of Love,* and is working on a science fantasy novel and her fifth full-length play.